Slow
Cooking

Slow Cooking

OVER 100 SLOW-COOKED RECIPES FOR
YOUR OVEN, STOVETOP OR SLOW COOKER

Bounty
BOOKS

An Hachette UK Company
www.hachette.co.uk

First published in Great Britain in 2016 by Bounty,
a division of Octopus Publishing Group Ltd
Carmelite House, 50 Victoria Embankment,
London EC4Y 0DZ
www.octopusbooks.co.uk

This material was previously published as *Mum's Favourite
Slow-Cooked Classics*

ISBN 978-0-7537-3125-3

A CIP catalogue record for this book is available from
the British Library

Printed and bound in China

10 9 8 7 6 5 4 3 2 1

Publisher: Lucy Pessell
Design Manager: Megan van Staden
Editor: Natalie Bradley
Production Controller: Paulina Stypińska

Contents

———

Introduction

————

This collection of slow-cooked classics offers a range of nostalgic, comforting recipes that are just the thing to banish the winter blues: warming soups, hearty stews and curries, delicious roasts, great side dishes, vegetarian options and sweetly indulgent puddings and cakes. There's also a chapter of recipes especially for making in your slow cooker.

Although you're sure to discover your own favourites, here are some suggestions for recipes for various occasions, such as when you are entertaining or have hungry children to feed.

GREAT MID-WEEK MEALS

Roast Chicken with Spiced Root Veg (see page 56)
Oxtail Stew (see page 91)
Chilli Con Carne (see page 32)
Fish Pie (see page 114)
Potato, Apple & Bacon Hotpot (see page 155)

KIDS' FAVOURITES

Steak & Kidney under a Hat (see page 94)
Home Baked Beans (see page 131)
Sausages with Onion Gravy (see page 164)
Chocolate Spotted Dick (see page 174)
Pineapple Pudding (see page 175)

HEALTHY OPTIONS

Vegetable Broth with Pearl Barley (see page 10)
Chicken Mulligatawny (see page 19)
Pumpkin & Root Vegetable Stew (see page 125)
Smoked Mackerel Kedgeree (see page 151)
Chicken, Vegetable & Lentil Stew (see page 81)

FOOD FOR FRIENDS

French Onion Soup (see page 24)
Roast Lamb with Wine & Juniper (see page 65)
Classic Coq au Vin (see page 77)
Potatoes Dauphinoise (see page 127)
Wicked Chocolate Pudding (see page 172)

STOCK

Many of the recipes in this book use stock. While good quality stock cubes or powder are convenient, making your own will give the finished dish a better flavour.

CHICKEN STOCK
Makes about 1 litre (1¾ pints)

1 leftover cooked chicken carcass
1 onion, quartered
2 carrots, thickly sliced
2 celery sticks, thickly sliced
1 bay leaf or a small bunch of mixed herbs
¼ teaspoon salt
½ teaspoon crushed black peppercorns
2.5 litres (4 pints) cold water

Put the carcass and vegetables into a large pan. Add the remaining ingredients and bring slowly just to the boil. Skim off any scum with a slotted spoon. Reduce the heat, half cover with a lid and simmer gently for 2–2½ hours until reduced by about half. Strain through a large sieve into a jug. Remove any meat still on the carcass, pick out the meat from the sieve and reserve for the stock, but discard the vegetables. Cool, then chill for several hours or overnight. Skim off any fat and then store in the refrigerator for up to 3 days or divide into freezerproof containers or plastic freezer bags and freeze for up to 6 months.

BEEF STOCK
Makes about 2.5 litres (4 pints)

2 kg (4 lb) beef bones, such as ribs or shin
2 smoked streaky bacon rashers, diced
2 onions, quartered
2 carrots, thickly sliced
2 celery sticks, thickly sliced
1 turnip, diced (optional)
2 bay leaves or rosemary sprigs
¼ teaspoon salt
½ teaspoon crushed black peppercorns
3.6 litres (6 pints) cold water

Put the bones and bacon in a large pan and heat gently for 10 minutes until the marrow begins to run from the centre of the bones. Turn the bones occasionally. Add the vegetables and fry for 10 minutes, stirring and turning the bones, until browned. Add the remaining ingredients and slowly bring to the boil. Skim off any scum with a slotted spoon. Reduce the heat, half cover with a lid and simmer gently for 4–5 hours until reduced by about half. Strain through a large sieve into a jug. Cool, then chill overnight. Skim off any fat and then store in the refrigerator for up to 3 days or divide into freezerproof containers or plastic freezer bags and freeze for up to 6 months.

VEGETABLE STOCK
Makes about 1 litre (1¾ pints)

1 tablespoon olive oil
2 onions, roughly chopped
2 leek tops, roughly chopped
4 carrots, thickly sliced
2 celery sticks, thickly sliced
100 g (3½ oz) cup mushrooms, sliced
4 tomatoes, roughly chopped
small bunch mixed herbs
¼ teaspoon salt
½ teaspoon crushed black peppercorns
1.8 litres (3 pints) cold water

Heat the oil in a large pan, add the vegetables and fry for 5 minutes until softened. Add the remaining ingredients and slowly bring to the boil. Reduce the heat, half cover with a lid and simmer gently for 1 hour. Strain through a large sieve into a jug. Cool, then store in the refrigerator for up to 3 days or divide into freezerproof containers or plastic freezer bags and freeze for up to 6 months.

Super Soups

Vegetable Broth with Pearl Barley
Guinea Fowl & Bean Soup
Turkey & Chestnut Soup
Beer Broth with Mini Meatballs
Simple Beef Soup
Chicken Mulligatawny
Split Pea & Parsnip Soup
Spanish Chickpea Soup
French Onion Soup
White Bean Soup Provençal
Venison, Red Wine & Lentil Soup
Goulash Soup

Vegetable Broth with Pearl Barley

SERVES 4 | PREPARATION TIME 15 minutes | COOKING TIME 1½ hours

100 g (3½ oz) pearl barley

2 tablespoons extra virgin rapeseed oil

1 large onion, finely chopped

2 leeks, trimmed, cleaned and finely chopped

1 celery stick, finely chopped

750 g (1½ lb) mixed root vegetables such as parsnips, swede, turnips, carrots and potatoes, evenly diced

1.2 litres (2 pints) beef or vegetable stock (see page 7)

1 bouquet garni

salt and pepper

1. Bring a large saucepan of water to the boil and pour in the pearl barley. Cook at a gentle simmer for 1 hour. Drain well.

2. Meanwhile, heat the oil in a large, heavy-based saucepan over a medium-low heat, add the onion, leeks and celery and fry gently for 8–10 minutes or until softened but not coloured. Add the root vegetables and cook for a further 5 minutes, stirring regularly.

3. Pour in the stock, add the bouquet garni and bring to the boil. Stir in the pearl barley, then reduce the heat and simmer for 25–30 minutes or until the vegetables and pearl barley are tender. Remove the bouquet garni and season to taste with salt and pepper before serving.

Guinea Fowl & Bean Soup

SERVES 4–6 | PREPARATION TIME 20 minutes, plus soaking | COOKING TIME 1½ hours

250 g (8 oz) dried black-eyed beans

1 kg (2 lb) oven-ready guinea fowl

1 onion, sliced

2 garlic cloves, crushed

1.5 litres (2½ pints) chicken stock (see page 7)

½ teaspoon ground cloves

50 g (2 oz) can anchovies, drained and finely chopped

100 g (3½ oz) watercress

150 g (5 oz) wild mushrooms

3 tablespoons tomato purée

salt and pepper

1. Put the beans in a bowl, cover with plenty of cold water and leave to soak overnight.

2. Drain the beans and put in a large saucepan. Cover with water and bring to the boil. Boil for 10 minutes, then drain the beans through a colander.

3. Put the guinea fowl in the pan and add the drained beans, onion, garlic, stock and cloves. Bring just to the boil, then reduce the heat to its lowest setting and cover with a lid. Cook very gently for 1¼ hours until the guinea fowl is very tender.

4. Drain the guinea fowl to a plate and leave until cool enough to handle. Flake all the meat from the bones, discarding the skin. Chop up any large pieces of meat and return all the meat to the pan.

5. Scoop a little of the stock into a small bowl with the anchovies and mix together so that the anchovies are blended with the stock. Discard the tough stalks from the watercress.

6. Add the anchovy mixture, mushrooms and tomato purée to the pan and season with salt and plenty of black pepper. Reheat gently for a few minutes and stir in the watercress just before serving.

Turkey & Chestnut Soup

———

SERVES 6 | PREPARATION TIME 20 minutes | COOKING TIME 3½ hours

1 turkey carcass

leftover stuffing (optional)

2 onions, finely chopped

2 carrots, finely chopped

2 celery sticks, finely chopped

1.8 litres (3 pints) water

cooked turkey, cut into
  bite-sized pieces

2 tablespoons oil

2 large potatoes, diced

475 g (15 oz) can whole
  chestnuts in brine, drained

3 tablespoons sherry or port

salt and pepper

1. Break the turkey carcass into pieces and place in a large saucepan with the stuffing, if using, and 1 onion, 1 carrot, 1 celery stick and the seasoning. Add the measurement water and bring to the boil. Cover and simmer for 3 hours. Add extra water as necessary.

2. Remove the carcass and vegetables and discard. Strain the stock and add the turkey meat.

3. Heat the oil in the rinsed-out pan, then add the potatoes and the remaining onion, carrot and celery. Cook gently, stirring, for 5 minutes.

4. Pour in the turkey stock and bring to the boil. Simmer for 20 minutes, then add the chestnuts and sherry or port. Reheat and check the seasoning before serving.

Beer Broth with Mini Meatballs

SERVES 6 | PREPARATION TIME 25 minutes | COOKING TIME about 1¼ hours

25 g (1 oz) butter

1 onion, chopped

200 g (7 oz) potato, diced

125 g (4 oz) swede or parsnip, diced

1 carrot, diced

2 tomatoes, skinned if liked, roughly chopped

½ lemon, sliced

900 ml (1½ pints) beef stock (see page 7)

450 ml (¾ pint) can lager

¼ teaspoon ground cinnamon

¼ teaspoon grated nutmeg

100 g (3½ oz) green cabbage, finely shredded

salt and pepper

MEATBALLS

250 g (8 oz) extra-lean minced beef

40 g (1½ oz) long-grain rice

3 tablespoons chopped parsley, plus extra to garnish

1. Heat the butter in a large saucepan, add the onion and fry gently for 5 minutes until just turning golden around the edges. Stir in the diced root vegetables, the tomatoes and lemon.

2. Pour in the stock and lager, then add the spices and season well with salt and pepper. Bring to the boil, stirring, then cover and simmer for 45 minutes.

3. Meanwhile, mix all the meatball ingredients together. Divide into 18 and shape into small balls with wetted hands. Chill until needed.

4. Add the meatballs to the soup, bring the soup back to the boil, then cover and simmer for 10 minutes. Add the cabbage and cook for 10 minutes until the cabbage is tender and the meatballs cooked all the way through. Taste and adjust the seasoning. Ladle into shallow bowls and sprinkle with a little chopped parsley, if liked.

Simple Beef Soup

———

SERVES 8 | PREPARATION TIME 25 minutes, plus cooling | COOKING TIME 2 hours

750 g (1½ lb) piece of topside or braising steak

250 g (8 oz) carrots, finely chopped

250 g (8 oz) leeks, finely chopped

4 celery sticks, finely chopped

125 g (4 oz) mushrooms, finely chopped

500 g (1 lb) potatoes, finely chopped

175 g (6 oz) white turnips, finely chopped

finely chopped parsley, to garnish

STOCK

2.5 litres (4 pints) water

1 carrot, roughly chopped

1 onion, halved, not peeled

1 celery stick, broken

1 leek, cut into 5 cm (2 inch) pieces

1 teaspoon cloves

1 teaspoon black peppercorns

¼ teaspoon salt

1 bouquet garni

1. Place all the stock ingredients in a large saucepan and bring to the boil. Add the beef, cover and simmer for 1½ hours, or until the beef is tender.

2. Remove the beef from the stock, allow to cool and dice finely. Strain the stock and discard the vegetables and bouquet garni. Return the strained stock to the cleaned saucepan. Add the prepared vegetables, cover and simmer for 15 minutes or until the vegetables are just tender. Add the diced beef and simmer for a further 5 minutes. Ladle into bowls and serve with a little finely chopped parsley.

Chicken Mulligatawny

_____

SERVES 6 | PREPARATION TIME 15 minutes | COOKING TIME about 1¼ hours

1 tablespoon sunflower oil

1 onion, finely chopped

1 carrot, diced

1 dessert apple, peeled, cored
  and diced

2 garlic cloves, finely chopped

250 g (8 oz) tomatoes, skinned
  if liked, roughly chopped

4 teaspoons medium curry
  paste

50 g (2 oz) sultanas

125 g (4 oz) red lentils

1.5 litres (2½ pints) chicken
  stock (see page 7)

125 g (4 oz) leftover cooked
  chicken, cut into shreds

salt and pepper

coriander sprigs, to garnish

1. Heat the oil in a saucepan, add the onion and carrot and fry for 5 minutes, stirring, until softened and just turning golden around the edges. Stir in the apple, garlic, tomatoes and curry paste and cook for 2 minutes.

2. Stir in the sultanas, lentils and stock. Season with salt and pepper and bring to the boil, cover and simmer for 1 hour until the lentils are soft. Mash the soup to make a coarse purée. Add the cooked chicken, heat thoroughly then taste and adjust the seasoning if needed. Ladle into bowls and garnish with coriander sprigs. Serve with warm naan bread or poppadums.

Split Pea & Parsnip Soup

SERVES 6 | PREPARATION TIME 20 minutes, plus soaking | COOKING TIME 1¼ hours

250 g (8 oz) yellow split peas, soaked overnight in cold water

300 g (10 oz) parsnips, cut into chunks

1 onion, roughly chopped

1.5 litres (2½ pints) chicken or vegetable stock (see page 7)

salt and pepper

CORIANDER BUTTER

1 teaspoon cumin seeds, roughly crushed

1 teaspoon coriander seeds, roughly crushed

2 garlic cloves, finely chopped

75 g (3 oz) butter

small bunch of coriander

1. Drain the soaked split peas and put them into a saucepan with the parsnips, onion and stock. Bring to the boil and boil for 10 minutes. Reduce the heat, cover and simmer for 1 hour or until the split peas are soft.

2. Meanwhile, make the butter by dry-frying the cumin and coriander seeds and garlic in a small saucepan until lightly toasted. Mix into the butter with the coriander leaves and a little salt and pepper. Shape into a sausage shape on clingfilm or foil, wrap up and chill until needed.

3. Roughly mash the soup or purée in batches in a liquidizer or food processor, if preferred. Reheat and stir in half the coriander butter until melted. Add a little extra stock if needed then season to taste. Ladle into bowls and top each bowl with a slice of the coriander butter.

Spanish Chickpea Soup

SERVES 8 | PREPARATION TIME 15 minutes, plus soaking | COOKING TIME 2¼ hours

150 g (5 oz) dried chickpeas, soaked for 48 hours in cold water or 12 hours in boiling water

500–750 g (1–1½ lb) boneless smoked bacon hock joint

1 onion, studded with 4 cloves

2 garlic cloves, crushed

1 bay leaf

sprig of thyme

sprig of marjoram

sprig of flat leaf parsley

1.8 litres (3 pints) water

1.8 litres (3 pints) chicken stock (see page 7)

300–375 g (10–12 oz) potatoes, cut into 1 cm (½ inch) cubes

300 g (10 oz) Savoy cabbage, shredded

salt and pepper

1. Drain the chickpeas, rinse under cold running water and drain again. Put the bacon joint in a large, deep saucepan and cover with cold water. Bring the water briefly to the boil, then drain, discarding the water.

2. Transfer the bacon joint to a clean, large heavy-based saucepan. Add the chickpeas, studded onion, garlic, bay leaf, thyme, marjoram, parsley and measurement water. Bring to the boil, then reduce the heat, partially cover and simmer for 1½ hours until the meat is tender.

3. Remove and discard the onion and herbs. Remove the hock, transfer to a board and cut into small pieces. Set aside. Add the stock, potatoes and cabbage to the pan, and simmer for a further 30 minutes.

4. Add the reserved hock pieces to the soup and cook for a further 10 minutes. Season with salt and pepper. Ladle into warm soup bowls and serve with fresh, crusty bread.

French Onion Soup

SERVES 4 | PREPARATION TIME 15 minutes | COOKING TIME 1 hour

25 g (1 oz) butter

2 tablespoons olive oil

500 g (1 lb) large onions,
  halved and thinly sliced

1 tablespoon caster sugar

3 tablespoons brandy

150 ml (¼ pint) red wine

1 litre (1¾ pints) beef stock
  (see page 7)

1 bay leaf

salt and pepper

CHEESY CROÛTES

4–8 slices French bread

1 garlic clove, halved

40 g (1½ oz) Gruyère cheese,
  grated

1. Heat the butter and oil in a saucepan, add the onions and toss in the butter, then fry very gently for 20 minutes, stirring occasionally until very soft and just beginning to turn golden around the edges.

2. Stir in the sugar and fry the onions for 20 minutes more, stirring more frequently towards the end of cooking until the onions are caramelized to a rich dark brown. Add the brandy and, when bubbling, flame with a long taper and quickly stand well back.

3. Add the wine, stock, bay leaf, salt and pepper as soon as the flames subside, then bring to the boil. Cover and simmer for 20 minutes. Taste and adjust the seasoning if needed.

4. For the cheesy croûtes, toast the bread on both sides then rub with the cut surface of the garlic. Sprinkle with the cheese and put back under the grill until the cheese is bubbling. Ladle the soup into bowls and top with the cheesy croûtes.

White Bean Soup Provençal

SERVES 6 | PREPARATION TIME 15 minutes, plus soaking | COOKING TIME 1¼–1¾ hours

3 tablespoons olive oil

2 garlic cloves, crushed

1 small red pepper, cored, deseeded and chopped

1 onion, finely chopped

250 g (8 oz) tomatoes, finely chopped

1 teaspoon finely chopped thyme

400 g (14 oz) can dried haricot or cannellini beans, soaked overnight in cold water, rinsed and drained

600 ml (1 pint) water

600 ml (1 pint) vegetable stock (see page 7)

2 tablespoons finely chopped flat leaf parsley

salt and pepper

1. Heat the oil in a large heavy-based saucepan, add the garlic, red pepper and onion and cook over a medium heat for 5 minutes or until softened.

2. Add the tomatoes and thyme and cook for 1 minute. Add the beans and pour in the measurement water and stock. Bring to the boil, then reduce the heat, cover and simmer for 1–1½ hours until the beans are tender (you may need to allow for a longer cooking time, depending on how old the beans are).

3. Sprinkle in the parsley and season with salt and pepper. Ladle the soup into warm soup bowls and serve with fresh, crusty bread.

Venison, Red Wine & Lentil Soup

SERVES 6 | PREPARATION TIME 20 minutes | COOKING TIME about 1½ hours

6 venison sausages

1 tablespoon olive oil

1 onion, roughly chopped

2 garlic cloves, finely chopped

200 g (7 oz) potatoes, diced

1 carrot, diced

4 tomatoes, skinned if liked, roughly chopped

125 g (4 oz) green lentils

300 ml (½ pint) red wine

1.5 litres (2½ pints) beef stock (see page 7) or pheasant stock

2 tablespoons cranberry sauce

1 tablespoon tomato purée

1 teaspoon ground allspice

thyme sprig

2 bay leaves

salt and pepper

TO SERVE

garlic croûtons (see page 77)

finely chopped parsley

1. Grill the sausages until browned and just cooked. Meanwhile heat the oil in a large saucepan, add the onion and fry for 5 minutes until softened and just beginning to brown. Add the garlic, potato and carrot and fry briefly, then mix in the tomatoes and lentils.

2. Pour in the wine and stock, then add the cranberry sauce, tomato purée, allspice and herbs. Season well with salt and pepper then slice the sausages and add these to the pan. Bring to the boil, stirring, then cover and simmer gently for 1¼ hours. Taste and adjust seasoning if needed. Ladle the soup into bowls and serve with garlic croûtons (see page 77) and sprinkled with parsley.

Goulash Soup

———

SERVES 6 | PREPARATION TIME 15 minutes | COOKING TIME 1¼ hours

3 tablespoons vegetable oil

750 g (1½ lb) boneless lean
    beef, cut into 2.5 cm (1 inch)
    strips

2 onions, chopped

2 garlic cloves, crushed

2 celery sticks, sliced

3 tablespoons paprika

1 tablespoon caraway seeds

1.2 litres (2 pints) beef stock
    (see page 7)

600 ml (1 pint) water

¼ teaspoon dried thyme

2 bay leaves

¼ teaspoon Tabasco sauce (or
    to taste)

3 tablespoons tomato purée

250 g (8 oz) potatoes, peeled
    and cut into 1 cm (½ inch)
    cubes

3 carrots, cut into 1 cm
    (½ inch) cubes

soured cream, to serve
    (optional)

1. Put the oil in a large heavy-based saucepan over a medium-high heat. When the oil is hot, add the beef, in batches to avoid crowding the pan, and cook for a few minutes until browned all over. As each batch browns, remove with a slotted spoon and drain on kitchen paper. Reduce the heat to medium and add the onions, garlic and celery to the pan. Cook for 5 minutes or until softened.

2. Remove from the heat and stir in the paprika and caraway seeds. Pour in the stock and measurement water. Add the thyme, bay leaves, Tabasco sauce and tomato purée. Stir well and add the browned beef.

3. Bring to the boil, then reduce the heat, partially cover and simmer for about 30 minutes.

4. Add the potatoes and carrots and simmer for another 30 minutes or until the beef and potatoes are tender. Remove and discard the bay leaves. Spoon the soup into warm soup bowls, garnish each portion with a dollop of soured cream, if liked, and serve immediately.

Something Spicy

Chilli Con Carne
Calcutta Beef Curry
Beef & Potato Madras
Slow-cooked Beef Curry
Curried Oxtail & Chickpea Stew
Lamb Rogan Josh
Turkish Lamb & Spinach Curry

Chilli Con Carne

———

SERVES 4 | PREPARATION TIME 15 minutes | COOKING TIME about 1¼ hours

2 tablespoons vegetable oil

2 onions, chopped

1 red pepper, cored, deseeded and cut into cubes

2 garlic cloves, crushed

500 g (1 lb) minced beef

450 ml (¾ pint) beef stock

½–1 teaspoon chilli powder

475 g (15 oz) canned red kidney beans, drained

400 g (13 oz) can chopped tomatoes

1 tablespoon tomato purée

1 teaspoon ground cumin

salt and pepper

250 g (8 oz) long-grain white rice

TO SERVE

soured cream

red chilli flakes

Cheddar cheese, grated

finely chopped spring onion

1. Heat the oil in a saucepan over a low heat. Add the onions and red pepper and gently fry, stirring now and then, for about 5 minutes until soft. Add the garlic and cook for another 1 minute until opaque.

2. Increase the heat slightly and add the meat. Fry until just brown, stirring and breaking up the meat with a wooden spoon. Pour in the stock, then add the chilli powder, beans, tomatoes, tomato purée, cumin and a dash of salt and pepper.

3. Bring to the boil, then cover, reduce the heat to as low as possible and simmer very gently for 50–60 minutes, stirring occasionally so that it does not stick to the bottom of the pan.

4. Cook the rice, towards the end of the chilli's cooking time, in lightly salted water, according to the packet instructions, then drain.

5. Pile up the rice on each of 4 warm serving plates, dollop on the cooked chilli and top with the soured cream. Scatter over the chilli flakes, grated Cheddar and spring onion and serve immediately.

Calcutta Beef Curry

———

SERVES 4 | PREPARATION TIME 20 minutes, plus marinating | COOKING TIME 1 hour 20 minutes

400 g (13 oz) stewing beef, cut into bite-sized pieces
5 tablespoons natural yogurt
1 tablespoon medium curry powder
2 tablespoons mustard oil
1 dried bay leaf
1 cinnamon stick
3 cloves
4 green cardamom pods, bruised
1 large onion, halved and thinly sliced
3 garlic cloves, crushed
1 teaspoon finely grated fresh root ginger
1 teaspoon ground turmeric
1 teaspoon hot chilli powder
2 teaspoons ground cumin
400 ml (14 fl oz) beef stock (see page 7)
salt

1. Place the meat in a non-metallic bowl. Mix together the yogurt and curry powder and pour over the meat. Season with salt, cover and marinate in the refrigerator for 24 hours.

2. Heat the oil in a large nonstick wok or frying pan and add the spices. Stir-fry for 1 minute and then add the onion. Stir-fry over a medium heat for 4–5 minutes, then add the garlic, ginger, turmeric, chilli powder and cumin. Add the marinated meat and stir-fry for 10–15 minutes over a low heat.

3. Pour in the beef stock and bring to the boil. Reduce the heat to low, cover tightly and simmer gently, stirring occasionally, for 1 hour or until the meat is tender. Check the seasoning, remove from the heat and serve immediately with rice and pickles, if liked.

Beef & Potato Madras

———

SERVES 4 | PREPARATION TIME 15 minutes, plus marinating | COOKING TIME 2–2½ hours

5 tablespoons fat-free natural yogurt

5 tablespoons Madras curry powder

625 g (1¼ lb) lean beef fillet, cubed

2 tablespoons groundnut oil

1 large onion, thinly sliced

3 garlic cloves, crushed

1 teaspoon peeled and finely grated fresh root ginger

2 potatoes, peeled and cut into 2.5 cm (1 inch) chunks

400 g (13 oz) can chopped tomatoes

400 ml (14 fl oz) beef stock (see page 7)

¼ teaspoon garam masala

salt

chopped coriander leaves, to garnish

1. Mix the yogurt with the curry powder in a large non-metallic bowl. Add the meat, toss to combine, season to taste and marinate in the refrigerator for 24 hours.

2. Heat the oil in a large nonstick wok or frying pan with a lid over a medium heat. Add the onion and stir-fry for 4–5 minutes until soft. Add the garlic and ginger, and stir-fry for a further 30 seconds.

3. Reduce the heat to low and add the meat. Stir-fry for 10–15 minutes. Add the potatoes, tomatoes and stock and bring to the boil. Reduce the heat to very low (using a heat diffuser if possible), cover the pan tightly and simmer gently for 1½–2 hours, stirring occasionally, until the meat is meltingly tender. Check the seasoning and adjust if necessary. Serve garnished with chopped coriander.

Slow-cooked Beef Curry

———

SERVES 4–6 | PREPARATION TIME 20 minutes | COOKING TIME 2¼ hours

1 tablespoon groundnut oil

1 large onion, chopped

750 g (1½ lb) stewing steak, cubed

2 tablespoons tomato purée

3 tomatoes, chopped

250 ml (8 fl oz) water

3 tablespoons natural yogurt, plus extra to serve

1 teaspoon nigella seeds

salt and pepper

CURRY PASTE

2 teaspoons cumin seeds

1 teaspoon coriander seeds

½ teaspoon fennel seeds

2 garlic cloves, chopped

1 tablespoon peeled and grated fresh root ginger

1–2 small fresh green chillies

1 teaspoon paprika

1 teaspoon ground turmeric

2 tablespoons tomato purée

2 tablespoons groundnut oil

25 g (1 oz) coriander leaves, plus extra to garnish

1. Place the whole spices for the curry paste in a small frying pan and dry-fry over a medium heat for 2–3 minutes until fragrant. Tip the contents of the pan into a mini blender and grind to a fine powder. Add the remaining curry paste ingredients and blend to a smooth paste.

2. Heat the oil in a large saucepan over a medium heat, add the onion and cook for 5–6 minutes or until beginning to colour, stirring occasionally. Add 3 tablespoons of the prepared curry paste and stir-fry for 1–2 minutes.

3. Stir in the beef and cook for 4–5 minutes or until the meat is browned and well coated. Stir in the tomato purée, tomatoes, measured water and yogurt, and bring to the boil. Reduce the heat, cover and simmer for 2 hours or until tender, adding more liquid if necessary.

4. Season to taste and ladle into warm bowls. Sprinkle with the nigella seeds and garnish with coriander leaves. Serve with naan bread and yogurt.

Curried Oxtail & Chickpea Stew

———

SERVES 4 | PREPARATION TIME 20 minutes | COOKING TIME about 3 hours

1.5 kg (3 lb) oxtail, cubed

1 tablespoon groundnut oil

2 teaspoons ground allspice

2 teaspoons medium curry
    powder

1.5 litres (2½ pints) beef stock
    (see page 7)

4 carrots, cut into chunks

2 onions, finely chopped

3 garlic cloves, finely chopped

2 thyme sprigs

1 fresh Scotch bonnet chilli

400 g (14 oz) can chopped
    tomatoes

4 tablespoons cornflour

400 g (14 oz) can chickpeas,
    rinsed and drained

salt and pepper

1. Bring a large saucepan of water to the boil. Add the oxtail and bring back to the boil. Reduce the heat and simmer for 10–12 minutes. Drain and pat dry with kitchen paper. Season to taste.

2. Heat the oil in a large saucepan or casserole and brown the oxtail on both sides for 6–8 minutes. Add the allspice, curry powder, beef stock, carrots, onion, garlic, thyme, chilli, tomatoes and cornflour. Stir to mix well and bring to the boil. Cover and simmer gently for 2½ hours or until the oxtail is meltingly tender.

3. Add the chickpeas and cook for a further 15 minutes. Serve the stew immediately with mashed potatoes.

Lamb Rogan Josh

SERVES 4 | PREPARATION TIME 20 minutes | COOKING TIME about 3 hours

2 tablespoons sunflower oil

625 g (1¼ lb) boneless lamb, cut into large chunks

2 large onions, thickly sliced

3 garlic cloves, crushed

2 teaspoons finely grated fresh root ginger

2 cinnamon sticks

6 green cardamom pods

4 tablespoons medium curry paste

400 g (13 oz) canned chopped tomatoes

6 tablespoons tomato purée

1 teaspoon sugar

400 ml (14 fl oz) lamb stock

4 potatoes, cut into chunks

salt and pepper

chopped fresh coriander, to garnish

natural yogurt, to serve (optional)

1. Heat half the oil in a large, heavy-based casserole dish and cook the lamb, in batches, for 3–4 minutes until browned, then remove with a slotted spoon and set aside.

2. Add the remaining oil to the dish and add the onions. Cook over a medium heat for 10–12 minutes, stirring often, until soft and lightly browned.

3. Add the garlic, ginger, cinnamon and cardamom pods. Stir-fry for 1–2 minutes and then add the curry paste and lamb. Stir-fry for 2–3 minutes and then stir in the tomatoes, tomato purée, sugar, stock and potatoes. Season well and bring to the boil.

4. Reduce the heat, cover and simmer very gently (using a heat diffuser if possible) for 2–2½ hours or until the lamb is tender. Remove from the heat and serve garnished with chopped fresh coriander and drizzled with yogurt, if liked.

Turkish Lamb & Spinach Curry

—

SERVES 4 | PREPARATION TIME 20 minutes | COOKING TIME 2 hours

4 tablespoons sunflower oil

600 g (1 lb 4 oz) boneless shoulder of lamb, cut into bite-sized pieces

1 onion, finely chopped

3 garlic cloves, crushed

1 teaspoon ground ginger

2 teaspoons ground turmeric

large pinch of grated nutmeg

4 tablespoons sultanas

1 teaspoon ground cinnamon

1 teaspoon paprika

400 g (13 oz) canned chopped tomatoes

300 ml (½ pint) lamb stock

400 g (13 oz) baby leaf spinach

salt and pepper

natural yogurt, to serve (optional)

1. Heat half the oil in a large, heavy-based saucepan and brown the lamb, in batches, for 3–4 minutes. Remove with a slotted spoon and set aside.

2. Heat the remaining oil in the pan and add the onion, garlic, ginger, turmeric, nutmeg, sultanas, cinnamon and paprika. Stir-fry for 1–2 minutes and then add the lamb. Stir-fry for 2–3 minutes and then add the tomatoes and stock. Season well and bring to the boil. Reduce the heat, cover tightly and simmer very gently (using a heat diffuser if possible) for 1½ hours.

3. Add the spinach in batches until it is all wilted, cover and cook for a further 10–12 minutes, stirring occasionally. Remove from the heat and serve drizzled with yogurt, if liked.

68

60

69

Favourite Roasts

Roast Turkey with Orange Stuffing
Stuffed Turkey Breast Joint
Roast Goose with Spiced Apples
Pot-roast Chicken with Vermouth
Roast Chicken with Spiced Root Veg
Roast Chicken with Herbs & Garlic
Chicken in a Pot
Silverside with Dumplings
Salt Beef with Spring Vegetables
Roast Lamb with Wine & Juniper
Loin of Pork with Lentils
Herbed Pork Belly
Pork Spare Ribs
Pot-roasted Pork with Prunes

Roast Turkey with Orange Stuffing

———

SERVES 10 | PREPARATION TIME 40 minutes, plus resting | COOKING TIME about 3½ hours

5 kg (11 lb) oven-ready turkey, giblets removed and cavity wiped clean

1 small onion, halved

40 g (1½ oz) butter, softened

2 tablespoons vegetable oil

3 thyme sprigs, chopped

salt and pepper

ORANGE STUFFING

75 g (3 oz) sugar

150 ml (¼ pint) water

grated rind and juice of 1 orange

250 g (8 oz) cranberries

75 g (3 oz) butter

1 large onion, finely chopped

375 g (12 oz) cooked mixed long-grain and wild rice

2 tablespoons chopped parsley

1 tablespoon chopped thyme

pinch of ground cloves

pinch of grated nutmeg

salt and pepper

1. To make the stuffing: put the sugar and water into a pan and stir over a low heat until the sugar is dissolved. Bring to the boil and boil for 2–3 minutes. Add the orange rind, juice and cranberries and stir with a wooden spoon, taking care not to crush the fruit. Simmer for 5 minutes until the sauce is translucent. Set aside. Melt the butter in a saucepan and fry the onion over a moderate heat for 3–4 minutes, stirring once or twice. Remove from the heat. Stir in the rice, herbs, spices and cranberry and orange mixture. Season with salt and pepper and set aside to cool.

2. Pack the stuffing loosely into the neck of the bird and secure the flap with 2 crossed skewers. Place the onion in the body cavity and season the cavity with salt and pepper. Tie the turkey legs together with string at the top of the drumsticks. Place the bird in a large roasting tin. Rub all over with softened butter and season. Add the oil to the tin. Cover loosely with foil and roast in a preheated oven, 190°C (375°F), Gas Mark 5, for 3 hours 10 minutes, basting from time to time. Remove the foil for the last 40 minutes of cooking to brown the bird and scatter over the chopped thyme. Check the turkey is cooked by inserting a skewer into the thickest part of the thigh. The juices should run clear. If pink, cook for a further 15 minutes and test again.

3. Transfer the turkey to a large dish, cover with clean foil and leave to rest for 15–20 minutes before carving. Arrange on a warm serving platter and serve with bacon-wrapped chipolatas, if liked.

Stuffed Turkey Breast Joint

SERVES 7–8 | PREPARATION TIME 30 minutes, plus resting | COOKING TIME about 2½ hours

3.5 kg (7½ lb) skin-on boned breast joint
125 g (4 oz) butter, softened
1 bay leaf
2 tablespoons vegetable oil
salt and pepper

APPLE & NUT STUFFING

1 tablespoon vegetable oil
½ large onion, finely chopped
1 celery stick, finely chopped
175 g (6 oz) mixed dried fruit, finely chopped
175 g (6 oz) fresh breadcrumbs
125 g (4 oz) mixed shelled nuts, finely chopped
½ medium cooking apple, peeled, cored and grated
1 tablespoon chopped parsley
½ tablespoon chopped thyme
1 egg, beaten

1. To make the stuffing: heat the oil in a pan, add the onion and celery and fry over a gentle heat, stirring frequently, for about 10 minutes until softened. Turn into a bowl, add the remaining stuffing ingredients with salt and pepper to taste and mix well together. Set aside.

2. Ease your fingers between the turkey skin and the breast meat. Push in the softened butter to cover the breast completely. Place the turkey skin side down, season with salt and pepper, then spread with the stuffing. Bring the turkey up and around the stuffing to enclose it, making as neat and compact a shape as possible, and secure with string. Tuck a bay leaf under the string.

3. Add the vegetable oil to the roasting tin, then place the turkey breast side up in the roasting tin. Cover loosely with foil and roast in a preheated oven, 190°C (375°F), Gas Mark 5, for 2 hours 20 minutes or until the juices run clear when the thickest part is pierced with a skewer. If the juices are pink, cook for a further 15 minutes and test again. Remove the foil for the last 40 minutes of cooking to brown the bird.

4. Lift the turkey out of the tin, cover tightly with foil and rest in a warm place for 15–20 minutes before serving. Place the turkey on a warm serving platter to serve.

Roast Goose with Spiced Apples

———

SERVES 8 | PREPARATION TIME 35 minutes | COOKING TIME 3¾ hours

5–6 kg (11–13 lb) oven-ready goose, plus giblets

1 onion, halved

1 carrot

1 celery stick

1.2 litres (2 pints) water

50 g (2 oz) butter

1 large onion, chopped

375 g (12 oz) dried figs, chopped

175 g (6 oz) fresh breadcrumbs

2 tablespoons chopped parsley

2 tablespoons chopped thyme

1 egg

8 small apples, cored

16 whole cloves

25 g (1 oz) light muscovado sugar

½ teaspoon ground mixed spice

salt and pepper

1. Put the giblets in a saucepan, discarding the liver. Add the halved onion, carrot, celery and measured water. Bring to the boil, reduce the heat and simmer gently for 1 hour. Strain the giblet stock and reserve.

2. Melt half the butter and fry the onion for 3 minutes. Remove from the heat and add 250 g (8 oz) of the figs and the breadcrumbs, parsley, thyme and egg. Season lightly and mix well. Pack half the stuffing into the neck end. Shape the remaining stuffing into 2.5 cm (1 inch) balls.

3. Tuck the skin flap under the bird and truss it, with the wings folded under the body and the legs tied together with string. Place on a rack over a roasting tin. Roast the goose in a preheated oven, 180°C (350°F), Gas Mark 4, for 2¾ hours.

4. Cut a thin slice off the top of each apple and discard. Stud each apple with 2 cloves. Combine the remaining figs, sugar and mixed spice and pack into the apples. Melt the remaining butter and pour it over the apples. Place the apples and stuffing in the oven 30 minutes before the end of the goose roasting time, basting the apples frequently with the butter. Test to see if the goose is cooked by inserting a skewer into the thickest part of the thigh. The juices should run clear. Transfer to a warm serving dish. Keep warm.

5. Pour off the fat from the roasting tin, add 600 ml (1 pint) reserved giblet stock, making up with water if necessary. Bring to the boil and season lightly with salt and pepper. Strain and serve with the goose.

Pot-roast Chicken with Vermouth

SERVES 4 | PREPARATION TIME 20 minutes | COOKING TIME 1 hour 40 minutes–1 hour 50 minutes

1 tablespoon olive oil

200 g (7 oz) shallots, peeled, halved

2 slices smoked back bacon, diced

2 garlic cloves, finely chopped

500 g (1 lb) baby new potatoes

25 g (1 oz) butter

1.5 kg (3 lb) whole chicken

4 stems celery, each cut into 3 sections

250 g (8 oz) baby carrots, large ones halved

3 bay leaves

200 ml (7 fl oz) dry vermouth

200 ml (7 fl oz) chicken stock (see page 7)

2 tablespoons chopped parsley, to garnish (optional)

salt and pepper

1. Heat the oil in a large flameproof casserole, add the shallots and bacon and fry for 3–4 minutes over a medium heat until just beginning to brown. Add the garlic and potatoes and fry until just beginning to colour. Tip on to a plate.

2. Add the butter to the pan and, when melted, add the chicken, breast side downwards. Fry each breast until golden, then turn over and fry the underside. Return the fried vegetables to the pan and tuck the celery and carrots around the sides of the chicken, adding the bay leaves and a little salt and pepper.

3. Pour in the vermouth and stock, then bring to the boil. Cover with a tight-fitting lid and transfer to a preheated oven, 190°C (375°F), Gas Mark 5, for 1¼ hours. Spoon the vermouth juices over the chicken, then cook uncovered for 20–30 minutes until golden and cooked through (test by inserting a skewer into the thickest part of the thigh – the juices should run clear).

4. Lift the chicken on to a serving plate, scoop the vegetables out with a draining spoon and nestle them around the chicken. Cover with foil and keep hot. Boil the remaining pan juices for about 5 minutes or until reduced by half, then pour into a jug and sprinkle the vegetables with the parsley, if liked. Carve and serve with the gravy.

Roast Chicken with Spiced Root Veg

———

SERVES 4 | PREPARATION TIME 30 minutes | COOKING TIME 1 hour 20 minutes

1.5 kg (3 lb) whole chicken
2 teaspoons coriander seeds
1 teaspoon fennel seeds
1 teaspoon cumin seeds
2 tablespoons olive oil
½ teaspoon turmeric
½ teaspoon paprika
2 parsnips
2 large carrots
2 sweet potatoes
1 large onion
8 garlic cloves, unpeeled
fresh coriander leaves, to
    garnish

GRAVY

2 tablespoons plain flour
450 ml (¾ pint) chicken stock
    (see page 7)

1. Place the chicken in a large roasting tin. Crush the seeds and put them in a large plastic bag with the oil, turmeric and paprika. Shake until well mixed. Spoon a little of the mixture over the chicken breast, then cover with foil. Roast the chicken in a preheated oven, 190°C (375°F), Gas Mark 5, for 1 hour 20 minutes.

2. Cut the vegetables into large chunks, add to the bag of spiced oil and toss. Add to the roasting tin after 20 minutes of cooking the chicken, tucking some garlic cloves between the chicken legs and adding the rest to the vegetables. Cook for 1 hour until golden, turning the vegetables after 30 minutes and removing the foil from the chicken at this point.

3. Transfer the chicken and vegetables from the roasting tin to a large serving plate and keep warm. Garnish with coriander.

4. Drain the fat from the meat juices and stir in the flour. To make the gravy, put the roasting tin on the hob and cook for 1 minute, stirring. Gradually stir in the stock and bring to the boil. Strain into a jug and serve immediately with the carved chicken and vegetables.

Roast Chicken with Herbs & Garlic

SERVES 4 | PREPARATION TIME 10 minutes | COOKING TIME about 1 hour

8 garlic cloves, unpeeled

4 large thyme sprigs

3 large rosemary sprigs

1 whole chicken, about
   1.75 kg (3½ lb)

1 tablespoon olive oil

salt and pepper

1. Put the garlic cloves and half the herb sprigs in the body cavity of the chicken. Pat the chicken dry with kitchen paper and rub the oil all over the outside of the bird. Strip the leaves off the remaining herb sprigs and rub over the bird, with a little salt and pepper.

2. Place the chicken, breast side up, in a roasting tin. Roast in a preheated oven, 220°C (425°F), Gas Mark 7, for 10 minutes. Turn the chicken over, breast side down, reduce the oven temperature to 180°C (350°F), Gas Mark 4, and cook for a further 20 minutes. Finally, turn the chicken back to its original position and roast for another 25 minutes until the skin is crisp and golden. Check that the chicken is cooked by piercing the thigh with a skewer. The juices should run clear, with no sign of pink. If not, cook for a further 10 minutes.

3. Transfer to a warm serving plate and leave to rest for 5 minutes before serving with the pan juices.

Chicken in a Pot

___

SERVES 4 | PREPARATION TIME 10 minutes | COOKING TIME 1½ hours

2 tablespoons olive oil

100 g (3½ oz) streaky bacon, chopped

2 onions, cut into wedges

500 g (1 lb) baby carrots, halved

600 g (1¼ lb) new potatoes, halved if large

1 garlic bulb, halved across the middle

bunch of thyme

1 fennel bulb, sliced

1.5 kg (3 lb) whole chicken

2 large glasses dry white wine

salt and pepper

1. Heat the oil in a large flameproof casserole, add the bacon and fry for 1–2 minutes until beginning to brown. Add all the remaining ingredients and season well.

2. Cover and place in a preheated oven, 200°C (400°F), Gas Mark 6, for 1 hour. Remove the lid and cook for a further 30 minutes or until the juices run clear when the thickest part of the leg is pierced with a skewer. Serve with large hunks of crusty bread, if liked.

Silverside with Dumplings

—

SERVES 6 | PREPARATION TIME 30 minutes | COOKING TIME 2–2½ hours

2 tablespoons olive oil

1.75–2 kg (3½–4 lb) silverside of beef, tied into a neat shape

1 onion, stuck with 6 cloves

1 bouquet garni

600 ml (1 pint) water

300 ml (½ pint) stout

12–16 pickling onions

500 g (1 lb) small carrots

DUMPLINGS

125 g (4 oz) self-raising flour

50 g (2 oz) shredded suet

2 tablespoons finely chopped flat leaf parsley

1 large egg, beaten with 4 tablespoons cold water

salt and pepper

1. Heat the oil in a large heavy-based saucepan and brown the meat. Add the onion, bouquet garni, measurement water and stout. Bring to the boil, then simmer for 1½ hours.

2. Carefully remove the onion and bouquet garni and add the onions and carrots. Bring to the boil and simmer for a further 15 minutes.

3. Meanwhile, make the dumplings. Sift the flour into a mixing bowl, add the suet and parsley, season and then mix to a dough with the egg and water. Roll the dough into small balls, drop into the simmering liquid in the saucepan and cook for 15 minutes.

4. Transfer the meat and vegetables to a warm serving dish. Strain some of the cooking liquid into a jug and serve with the carved meat and vegetables.

Salt Beef with Spring Vegetables

SERVES 6 | PREPARATION TIME 10 minutes, plus resting | COOKING TIME 2½ hours

1.75 kg (3½ lb) piece of salted and rolled brisket or silverside of beef

1 onion

15 whole cloves

300 g (10 oz) baby onions or shallots, peeled but left whole

3 bay leaves

plenty of thyme and parsley sprigs

½ teaspoon ground allspice

300 g (10 oz) small carrots

1 small swede, cut into small chunks

500 g (1 lb) floury potatoes, cut into chunks

pepper

chopped parsley, to garnish

1. Put the beef in a flameproof casserole in which it fits quite snugly. Stud the onion with the cloves and add to the casserole with the baby onions or shallots, bay leaves, herbs, allspice and plenty of pepper.

2. Add just enough water to cover the beef and bring slowly to the boil. Cover with a lid and place in a preheated oven, 120°C (250°F), Gas Mark ½, for 2½ hours or until the meat is tender, adding the carrots, swede and potatoes to the casserole after 1 hour of the cooking time. Leave to rest for 15 minutes before carving.

3. Drain the meat to a plate or board. Cut into thin slices and serve on warm plates with the vegetables. Sprinkle with parsley and serve with a jug of the cooking juices for pouring over.

Roast Lamb with Wine & Juniper

———

SERVES 6 | PREPARATION TIME 20 minutes | COOKING TIME 1 hour 35 minutes

2 tablespoons olive oil

1 leg of lamb, about 1.5 kg
  (3 lb), trimmed of excess fat

10 juniper berries, crushed

3 garlic cloves, crushed

50 g (2 oz) salted anchovies,
  boned and rinsed

1 tablespoon chopped
  rosemary

2 tablespoons balsamic
  vinegar

2 rosemary sprigs

300 ml (½ pint) dry white wine

salt and pepper

1. Heat the oil in a roasting tin in which the lamb will fit snugly. Add the lamb and cook until browned all over. Leave to cool.

2. Pound 6 of the juniper berries, the garlic, anchovies and chopped rosemary with the end of a rolling pin in a bowl. Stir in the vinegar and mix to a paste. Make small incisions all over the lamb with a small, sharp knife. Spread the paste over the lamb, working it into the incisions. Season with salt and pepper. Put the rosemary sprigs in the roasting tin and put the lamb on top. Pour in the wine and add the remaining juniper berries.

3. Cover the roasting tin with foil and bring to the boil, then cook in a preheated oven, 160°C (325°F), Gas Mark 3, for 1 hour, turning the lamb every 20 minutes. Raise the temperature to 200°C (400°F), Gas Mark 6, uncover and roast for a further 30 minutes until the lamb is very tender.

Loin of Pork
with Lentils

———

SERVES 5–6 | PREPARATION TIME 15 minutes, plus resting | COOKING TIME about 1 hour 55 minutes

175 g (6 oz) Puy lentils

875 g (1¾ lb) pork loin, rind removed, boned and rolled

2 tablespoons olive oil

2 large onions, sliced

3 garlic cloves, sliced

1 tablespoon finely chopped rosemary

300 ml (½ pint) chicken or vegetable stock (see page 7)

250 g (8 oz) baby carrots, scrubbed and left whole

salt and pepper

1. Put the lentils in a saucepan, cover with water and bring to the boil. Boil rapidly for 10 minutes, then drain well.

2. Sprinkle the pork with salt and pepper. Heat the oil in a large heavy-based frying pan and brown the meat on all sides. Transfer to a casserole dish and add the lentils.

3. Add the onions to the pan and fry for 5 minutes. Stir in the garlic, rosemary and stock and bring to the boil. Pour over the meat and lentils and cover with a lid. Place in a preheated oven, 180°C (350°F), Gas Mark 4, for 1 hour.

4. Stir the carrots into the casserole, season well and return to the oven for a further 20–30 minutes until the pork is cooked through and the lentils are soft. Drain the meat, transfer to a serving platter and leave to rest in a warm place for 20 minutes. Carve into thin slices, then serve with the lentils, carrots and juices.

Herbed Pork Belly

SERVES 4–6 | PREPARATION TIME 15 minutes, plus resting | COOKING TIME 1 hour 50 minutes

10 sage leaves

2 large rosemary sprigs

3 garlic cloves, crushed

1 tablespoon fennel seeds

4 tablespoons olive oil

1 boned pork belly joint, about 1.25 kg (2½ lb)

salt and pepper

1. Roughly chop the sage and rosemary and combine with the garlic, fennel seeds and half the oil in a small bowl.

2. Place the pork on a chopping board, skin side up, and score the rind at 2.5 cm (1 inch) intervals. Turn the meat over, skin side down, and season with salt and pepper. Rub the herb mixture all over the flesh. Roll the pork up and tie it tightly with string. Rub the skin all over with the remaining oil and a generous amount of salt.

3. Roast in a preheated oven, 220°C (425°F), Gas Mark 7, for 20 minutes, then reduce the temperature to 160°C (325°F), Gas Mark 3, and roast for a further 1½ hours. Leave the meat to rest for 10 minutes before carving and serving.

Pork Spare Ribs

Serve 4 | PREPARATION TIME 5 minutes | COOKING TIME 1 hour

2 pork spare rib racks (about
   1 kg (2 lb) each)
100 ml (3½ fl oz) tomato
   ketchup
2 tablespoons clear honey
1 tablespoon dark soy sauce
1 tablespoon olive oil
1 tablespoon malt vinegar
2 teaspoons Dijon mustard
salt and pepper

1. Arrange the ribs on a wire rack in a large roasting tin. Combine the remaining ingredients in a bowl. Brush the ribs generously on both sides with the marinade.

2. Roast the ribs in a preheated oven, 200°C (400°F), Gas Mark 6, for 30 minutes. Baste the ribs again on both sides with the marinade, using a clean brush, and roast for a further 30 minutes until golden and sticky.

3. Remove from the oven, brush over the remaining marinade and leave to cool for 5 minutes before serving, divided into 4 portions.

Pot-roasted Pork with Prunes

SERVES 5–6 | PREPARATION TIME 20 minutes, plus resting | COOKING TIME 2 hours

1 kg (2 lb) skinned, boned and rolled loin of pork
25 g (1 oz) butter
1 tablespoon olive oil
3 tablespoons mustard seeds
2 onions, sliced
4 garlic cloves, crushed
2 celery sticks, sliced
1 tablespoon plain flour
1 tablespoon chopped thyme
300 ml (½ pint) white wine
150 g (5 oz) pitted prunes, halved
500 g (1 lb) small new potatoes
2 tablespoons chopped mint
salt and pepper

1. Rub the pork with salt and pepper. Melt the butter with the oil in a large, flameproof casserole and sear the pork on all sides. Drain to a plate.

2. Add the mustard seeds and onions and fry for about 5 minutes until beginning to colour. Stir in the garlic and celery and cook for 2 minutes. Add the flour and cook, stirring for 1 minute.

3. Stir in the thyme, wine and seasoning and let the mixture bubble up. Return the pork to the pan and cover with a lid. Transfer to a preheated oven, 160°C (325°F), Gas Mark 3, for 45 minutes.

4. Stir the prunes, potatoes and mint into the cooking juices around the pork and return to the oven for a further 1 hour until the potatoes are very tender. Leave to rest for 15 minutes before serving.

95

79

98

88

Stews & Casseroles

Chicken with 30 Garlic Cloves
Classic Coq au Vin
Chicken with Spring Vegetables
Moroccan-style Chicken
Chicken, Vegetable & Lentil Stew
Italian Chicken with Tomato Sauce
Spring Braised Duck
Game & Chestnut Casserole
Rabbit in White Wine & Rosemary
Beef & Winter Veg Casserole
Beef, Pumpkin & Ginger Stew
Daube of Beef
Steak & Kidney under a Hat
Beef in Red Wine
Oxtail Stew
Beef Goulash
Beef & Cabbage with Caraway Dumplings
Creamy Pork & Cider Hotpot
Catalan Pork Stew
Pork, Leek & Apple Casserole
Lamb Hotpot with Dumplings
Lamb & Lemon Cobbler
Irish Stew

Chicken with 30 Garlic Cloves

SERVES 4 | PREPARATION TIME 25 minutes | COOKING TIME 1½ hours

---

4 chicken leg and thigh joints

25 g (1 oz) butter

1 tablespoon olive oil

250 g (8 oz) shallots, halved if large

2 tablespoons plain flour

200 ml (7 fl oz) dry white wine

200 ml (7 fl oz) chicken stock (see page 7)

2 teaspoons Dijon mustard

3 garlic bulbs

small bunch thyme

4 tablespoons crème frâiche (optional)

salt and pepper

---

1. Heat the butter with the oil in a large frying pan and fry the chicken until golden brown on both sides. Transfer to a large casserole dish.

2. Fry the shallots until softened and lightly browned. Stir in the flour, then gradually mix in the wine, stock, mustard and seasoning. Bring to the boil, stirring.

3. Separate the garlic cloves but do not peel them. Count out 30 cloves and add to the casserole dish with 3–4 thyme stems. Pour over the wine mix, then cover and cook in a preheated oven, 180°C (350°F), Gas Mark 4, for 1½ hours. Stir in the crème fraîche, if liked.

Classic Coq au Vin

———

SERVES 4 | PREPARATION TIME 25 minutes | COOKING TIME 1 hour 20 minutes

25 g (1 oz) plain flour

8 mixed chicken thigh and drumstick joints

2 tablespoons olive oil

375 g (12 oz) shallots, halved if large

125 g (4 oz) smoked streaky bacon

2 garlic cloves, finely chopped

4 tablespoons brandy or cognac

300 ml (½ pint) cheap burgundy red wine

200 ml (7 fl oz) chicken stock (see page 7)

2 teaspoons tomato purée

fresh or dried bouquet garni

salt and pepper

GARLIC CROÛTONS

25 g (1 oz) butter

1 tablespoon olive oil

1 garlic clove, finely chopped

½ stick French bread, thinly sliced

1. Mix the flour on a plate with a little seasoning, then use to coat the chicken joints. Heat the oil in a large shallow flameproof casserole (or frying pan and transfer chicken to a casserole dish later), add the chicken and cook over a high heat until golden on all sides. Lift out on to a plate.

2. Fry the shallots and bacon until golden, then stir in the garlic and return the chicken to the casserole. Pour over the brandy or cognac and when bubbling flame with a long taper. As soon as the flames subside, pour in the red wine and stock, then mix in the tomato purée and bouquet garni. Season, then cover the casserole and transfer to a preheated oven, 180°C (350°F), Gas Mark 4, and cook for 1¼ hours until tender.

3. When the chicken is cooked, pour the liquid from the casserole into a saucepan and boil for 5 minutes to reduce and thicken slightly. Return the liquid to the casserole.

4. For the garlic croûtons, heat the butter and oil in a frying pan, add the garlic and cook for 1 minute. Add the bread slices in a single layer and fry on both sides until golden. Serve coq au vin in shallow bowls topped with the garlic croûtons.

Chicken with Spring Vegetables

___

SERVES 4 | PREPARATION TIME 10 minutes, plus resting | COOKING TIME about 1¼ hours

1.5 kg (3 lb) chicken

about 1.5 litres (2½ pints) hot chicken stock (see page 7)

2 shallots, halved

2 garlic cloves

2 sprigs of parsley

2 sprigs of marjoram

2 sprigs of lemon thyme

2 carrots, halved

1 leek, trimmed and sliced

200 g (7 oz) tenderstem broccoli

250 g (8 oz) asparagus, trimmed

½ Savoy cabbage, shredded

1. Put the chicken in a large saucepan and pour over enough stock just to cover the chicken. Push the shallots, garlic, herbs, carrots and leek into the pan and place over a medium-high heat. Bring to the boil, then reduce the heat and simmer gently for 1 hour or until the chicken is falling away from the bones. Add the remaining vegetables to the pan and simmer for a further 6–8 minutes or until the vegetables are cooked.

2. Turn off the heat and leave to rest for 5–10 minutes before serving the chicken and vegetables in deep bowls with spoonfuls of the broth. Remove the skin, if preferred, and serve with plenty of crusty bread.

Moroccan-style Chicken

SERVES 4 | PREPARATION TIME 20 minutes, plus marinating | COOKING TIME 1 hour 40 minutes

8 large skinless chicken thighs
   or 1 whole chicken, jointed
1 teaspoon ground cumin
1 teaspoon ground coriander
½ teaspoon ground turmeric
1 teaspoon ground ginger
1 teaspoon paprika
3 tablespoons olive oil
2 onions, cut into wedges
2 garlic cloves, finely sliced
1 fennel bulb, sliced
300 g (10 oz) small new
   potatoes
handful of sultanas
8 ready-to-eat dried apricots
100 g (3½ oz) green olives
   (optional)
pinch of saffron threads
400 ml (14 fl oz) hot chicken
   stock (see page 7)
small bunch of coriander,
   chopped
salt and pepper

1. Slash each piece of chicken 2–3 times with a small knife. Mix together the spices and half the olive oil, rub over the chicken pieces, cover and marinate in the refrigerator for at least 2 hours, preferably overnight.

2. Heat the remaining oil in a large flameproof casserole, add the chicken pieces and fry for 4–5 minutes until golden all over. Add the onion, garlic and fennel to the pan and continue to fry for 2–3 minutes. Add all the remaining ingredients, except the coriander, and stir well.

3. Cover and simmer for 1½ hours or until the chicken begins to fall off the bone. Season well and stir in the coriander.

Chicken, Vegetable & Lentil Stew

———

SERVES 6 | PREPARATION TIME 15 minutes | COOKING TIME 2 hours

1 kg (2 lb) skinless chicken
  thigh fillets, halved
2 tablespoons plain flour,
  seasoned
3 tablespoons olive oil
1 large onion, chopped
2 carrots, chopped
2 celery sticks, chopped
2 garlic cloves, crushed
150 ml (¼ pint) dry white wine
1 litre (1¾ pints) chicken stock
  (see page 7)
1 tablespoon chopped
  rosemary
150 g (5 oz) Puy lentils
salt and pepper

1. Dust the chicken thighs with the seasoned flour to coat lightly.

2. Heat half the oil in a flameproof casserole, add the chicken, in 2 batches, and cook over a medium-high heat for 5 minutes until browned on both sides. Remove from the pan with a slotted spoon.

3. Reduce the heat to medium and add the remaining oil to the pan. Add the onion, carrots, celery, garlic and salt and pepper to taste and cook, stirring frequently, for 5 minutes. Add the wine, stock, rosemary and lentils and return the chicken thighs to the pan.

4. Bring to the boil, stirring, then reduce the heat, cover and simmer gently for 1½ hours until the vegetables and lentils are tender.

Italian Chicken with Tomato Sauce

___

SERVES 4 | PREPARATION TIME 20 minutes | COOKING TIME 1¼ hours

4 chicken legs, halved through
  the joints

4 tablespoons olive oil

1 large onion, finely chopped

1 celery stick, finely chopped

75 g (3 oz) pancetta, diced

2 garlic cloves, crushed

3 bay leaves

4 tablespoons dry vermouth
  or white wine

2 x 400 g (13 oz) cans
  chopped tomatoes

1 teaspoon caster sugar

3 tablespoons sun-dried
  tomato paste

25 g (1 oz) basil leaves, torn
  into pieces

8 black olives

salt and pepper

1. Season the chicken pieces with salt and pepper. Heat the oil in a large saucepan or sauté pan and fry the chicken pieces on all sides to brown. Drain to a plate.

2. Add the onion, celery and pancetta to the pan and fry gently for 10 minutes. Add the garlic and bay leaves and fry for a further 1 minute.

3. Add the vermouth or wine, tomatoes, sugar, tomato paste and seasoning and bring to the boil. Return the chicken pieces to the pan and reduce the heat to its lowest setting. Cook very gently, uncovered, for about 1 hour or until the chicken is very tender.

4. Stir in the basil and olives and check the seasoning before serving.

Spring Braised Duck

———

SERVES 4 | PREPARATION TIME 20 minutes | COOKING TIME 1¾ hours

4 duck legs

2 teaspoons plain flour

25 g (1 oz) butter

1 tablespoon olive oil

2 onions, sliced

2 streaky bacon rashers, finely chopped

2 garlic cloves, crushed

1 glass white wine, about 150 ml (¼ pint)

300 ml (½ pint) chicken stock (see page 7)

3 bay leaves

500 g (1 lb) small new potatoes

200 g (7 oz) fresh peas

150 g (5 oz) asparagus tips

2 tablespoons chopped mint

salt and pepper

1. Halve the duck legs through the joints. Mix the flour with a little seasoning and use to coat the duck pieces.

2. Melt the butter with the oil in a sturdy roasting pan or flameproof casserole and gently fry the duck pieces for about 10 minutes until browned. Drain to a plate and pour off all but 1 tablespoon of the fat left in the pan.

3. Add the onions and bacon to the pan and fry gently for 5 minutes. Add the garlic and fry for a further 1 minute. Add the wine, stock and bay leaves and bring to the boil, stirring. Return the duck pieces and cover with a lid or foil. Place in a preheated oven, 160°C (325°F), Gas Mark 3, for 45 minutes.

4. Add the potatoes to the pan, stirring them into the juices. Sprinkle with salt and return to the oven for 30 minutes. Add the peas, asparagus and mint to the pan and return to the oven for a further 15 minutes or until all the vegetables are tender. Check the seasoning and serve.

Game & Chestnut Casserole

─────

SERVES 6 | PREPARATION TIME 40 minutes | COOKING TIME 1 hour 40 minutes

500 g (1 lb) pork sausage meat
3 onions, finely chopped
2 tablespoons chopped thyme
400 g (13 oz) mixed game
350 g (12 oz) mixed poultry
2 tablespoons plain flour
100 g (3½ oz) butter
2 celery sticks, chopped
2 garlic cloves, crushed
750 ml (1¼ pints) chicken
   stock (see page 7) or game
   stock
10 juniper berries, crushed
200 g (7 oz) self-raising flour
1 teaspoon baking powder
Approx 150 ml (½ pint) milk,
   plus a little extra to glaze
200 g (7 oz) vacuum-packed
   prepared chestnuts
3 tablespoons Worcestershire
   sauce
salt and pepper

1. Mix the sausage meat with one-third of the onions, half the thyme and plenty of seasoning. Shape into balls about 1.5 cm (¾ inch) in diameter.

2. Cut all the meat into small pieces. Season the plain flour and use to coat the meat. Melt 25 g (1 oz) of the butter in a large, flameproof casserole and brown the meat in batches, draining each batch to a plate.

3. Melt another 25 g (1 oz) of the butter and fry the remaining onions and the celery for 5 minutes. Add the garlic and fry for 1 minute. Stir in any remaining coating flour, then blend in the stock. Return the meat to the pan with the juniper berries. Cover and place in a preheated oven, 160°C (325°F), Gas Mark 3, for 1 hour until the meat is tender.

4. Meanwhile, put the self-raising flour and baking powder in a food processor with a little salt, the remaining thyme and the remaining butter, cut into pieces. Blend to breadcrumb consistency. Add most of the milk to make a dough, adding the rest if it is very dry. Turn out on to a floured surface and roll out to 1.5 cm (¾ inch) thick. Cut out rounds using a 4 cm (1¾ inch) cutter.

5. Stir the chestnuts and the Worcestershire sauce into the casserole and check the seasoning. Arrange the scones around the edge and glaze with milk. Raise the oven temperature to 220°C (425°F), Gas Mark 7, and cook for 20 minutes or until the scones are cooked through.

Rabbit in White Wine & Rosemary

SERVES 4–6 | PREPARATION TIME 15 minutes | COOKING TIME 2 hours

25 g (1 oz) butter

3 tablespoons olive oil

1 rabbit, about 1.5 kg (3 lb), cut into joints (ask your butcher to do this for you)

2 onions, thinly sliced

1 small celery stick, finely diced

pinch of crushed dried chillies

3 large rosemary sprigs

1 lemon, quartered

12 black olives

350 ml (12 fl oz) dry white wine

250 ml (8 fl oz) chicken stock (see page 7)

salt

1. Melt half the butter with the oil in a large, flameproof casserole with a tight-fitting lid large enough to hold the rabbit in a single layer. Lightly season the rabbit with salt and add to the pan with the onions, celery, crushed chillies and rosemary. Cover and cook over a low heat for 1½ hours, turning the rabbit pieces every 30 minutes.

2. Uncover the pan, increase the heat to high and boil until most of the juices released by the rabbit during cooking have evaporated. Add the lemon and olives, stir well, then pour in the wine. Bring to the boil and boil for 2 minutes, for the alcohol to evaporate. Pour in the stock and simmer, turning and basting the rabbit occasionally, for a further 10–12 minutes until you have a rich, syrupy sauce. Serve hot.

Beef & Winter Veg Casserole

SERVES 4–6 | PREPARATION TIME 20 minutes | COOKING TIME 2 hours

25 g (1 oz) butter

750 g (1½ lb) stewing steak, cut into 1.5 cm (¾ inch) cubes

750 g (1½ lb) potatoes, peeled and diced

375 g (12 oz) carrots, diced

375 g (12 oz) swede, diced

375 g (12 oz) celeriac, diced

1 large onion, peeled and thinly sliced

600 ml (1 pint) bitter beer

600 ml (1 pint) beef stock (see page 7)

2 bay leaves

2 tablespoons tomato purée

1. Melt the butter in a large flameproof casserole over a high heat. Add the beef and brown on all sides, turning occasionally. Remove the beef from the casserole with a slotted spoon.

2. Lower the heat and add all the vegetables. Cover and cook over a low heat for 10 minutes. Pour in the beer and the stock and bring to the boil, then add the bay leaves and tomato purée. Return the meat to the casserole, cover and cook in a preheated oven, 180°C (350°F), Gas Mark 4, for 1½ hours, or until the meat is tender.

Beef, Pumpkin & Ginger Stew

SERVES 6 | PREPARATION TIME 20 minutes | COOKING TIME 1½ hours

2 tablespoons plain flour

750 g (1½ lb) lean stewing beef, diced

25 g (1 oz) butter

3 tablespoons vegetable oil

1 onion, chopped

2 carrots, sliced

2 parsnips, sliced

3 bay leaves

several thyme sprigs

2 tablespoons tomato purée

625 g (1¼ lb) pumpkin, peeled, deseeded and cut into small chunks

1 tablespoon dark muscovado sugar

50 g (2 oz) fresh root ginger, peeled and finely chopped

small handful of flat leaf parsley, chopped, plus extra to garnish

salt and pepper

1. Season the flour with salt and pepper and use to coat the beef. Melt the butter with the oil in a large saucepan over a medium-high heat. When the butter is foaming, fry the meat in 2 batches until browned all over, draining with a slotted spoon. Set aside on a plate.

2. Reduce the heat, add the onion, carrots and parsnips to the saucepan and fry gently for 5 minutes until softened but not coloured.

3. Return the meat to the pan and add the bay leaves, thyme and tomato purée. Pour in just enough water to cover the ingredients and bring slowly to the boil. Reduce the heat to its lowest setting, cover and simmer very gently for 45 minutes.

4. Add the pumpkin, sugar, ginger and parsley and simmer gently for a further 30 minutes until the pumpkin is soft and the meat is tender. Check the seasoning, adding salt and pepper if needed, and serve scattered with extra parsley.

Daube of Beef

SERVES 5–6 | PREPARATION TIME 20 minutes | COOKING TIME 1½ hours

1 tablespoon plain flour

1 kg (2 lb) braising beef, diced

4 tablespoons olive oil

100 g (3½ oz) streaky bacon, chopped

1 large onion, chopped

4 garlic cloves, crushed

several pared strips of orange rind

200 g (7 oz) carrots, sliced

several thyme sprigs

300 ml (½ pint) red wine

300 ml (½ pint) beef stock (see page 7)

100 g (3½ oz) pitted black olives

4 tablespoons sun-dried tomato paste

salt and pepper

1. Season the flour with salt and pepper and use to coat the beef. Heat the oil in a large, flameproof casserole and fry the meat in batches until browned, draining each batch to a plate. Add the bacon and onion to the casserole and fry for 5 minutes.

2. Return all the meat to the casserole with the garlic, orange rind, carrots, thyme sprigs, wine and stock. Bring almost to the boil, then cover with a lid and transfer to a preheated oven, 160°C (325°F), Gas Mark 3, for 1¼ hours or until the meat is very tender.

3. Put the olives and sun-dried tomato paste in a blender or food processor and blend very lightly until the olives are chopped but not puréed. Stir into the casserole and return to the oven for a further 15 minutes. Check the seasoning before serving.

Steak & Kidney under a Hat

SERVES 4 | PREPARATION TIME 25 minutes | COOKING TIME 1¾ hours

40 g (1½ oz) butter

750 g (1½ lb) steak and kidney, diced

4 tablespoons wholemeal flour, seasoned

1 large onion, thinly sliced

250 g (8 oz) flat mushrooms, thinly sliced

250 g (8 oz) white turnips, cubed

4 stalks celery, diced

600 ml (1 pint) beef stock (see page 7)

2 tablespoons Worcestershire sauce

1 bay leaf

1 tablespoon chopped thyme

1 tablespoon chopped parsley

salt and pepper

HAT

250 g (8 oz) wholemeal flour

2 teaspoons mustard powder

1 teaspoon dried thyme

½ teaspoon salt

1 teaspoon bicarbonate of soda

125 g (4 oz) shredded suet

150 ml (¼ pint) water

1. Coat the steak and kidney in the seasoned flour. Melt half the butter in a large heavy-bottomed saucepan over a high heat. Add the steak and kidney and brown on all sides. Remove from the saucepan with a slotted spoon.

2. Lower the heat, add the rest of the butter to the saucepan and add the onion, mushroom, turnip and celery. Cover the saucepan and cook gently for 5 minutes. Add the stock, Worcestershire sauce and herbs and bring to the boil.

3. Take off the heat, transfer to a large pie dish and cook in a preheated oven, 180°C (350°F), Gas Mark 4, for 1¼ hours.

4. Make the 'hat'. Place the flour, mustard powder, thyme, salt, bicarbonate of soda and suet in a mixing bowl. Add the measurement water and mix to a dough. Roll out the dough on a lightly floured board to a shape and size to cover the pie dish exactly.

5. Place it carefully on top of the steak and kidney mixture and return to the oven to cook for a further 20 minutes or until the hat becomes firm and just begins to colour. Serve immediately straight from the pie dish.

Beef in Red Wine

SERVES 4 | PREPARATION TIME 10 minutes | COOKING TIME 2¼ hours

875 g (1¾ lb) brisket of beef, cut into 5 cm (2 inch) pieces

1 celery stick

2 bay leaves

750 ml (1¼ pint) bottle full-bodied red wine

300 ml (½ pint) beef or chicken stock (see page 7)

2 carrots, cut at an angle into 3.5 cm (1½ inch) slices

20 baby onions, peeled but kept whole

salt and pepper

1. Season the beef with salt and pepper and put in a large, flameproof casserole with a tight-fitting lid. Add the celery and bay leaves, then pour in the wine and stock. Bring to the boil, then reduce the heat to a barely visible simmer and cook, covered, for 1½ hours, stirring occasionally.

2. Add the carrots and onions. Re-cover and simmer gently for a further 45 minutes, adding a little water if the sauce becomes too thick.

3. Remove the beef from the heat and serve accompanied with mashed potatoes.

Oxtail Stew

SERVES 4 | PREPARATION TIME 20 minutes | COOKING TIME 3¾ hours

2 tablespoons plain flour

1 tablespoon mustard powder

1 teaspoon celery salt

2 kg (4 lb) oxtail

50 g (2 oz) butter

2 tablespoons oil

2 onions, sliced

3 large carrots, sliced

3 bay leaves

100 g (3½ oz) tomato purée

100 ml (3½ fl oz) dry sherry

1 litre (1¾ pints) beef stock
  or vegetable stock (see
  page 7)

salt and pepper

1. Mix together the flour, mustard powder and celery salt on a large plate and use to coat the oxtail pieces.

2. Melt half the butter with 1 tablespoon of the oil in a large, flameproof casserole. Brown the oxtail, half at a time, and drain to a plate.

3. Add the onions and carrots to the pan with the remaining butter and oil. Fry until beginning to brown. Return the oxtail to the pan with the bay leaves and any remaining flour left on the plate.

4. Mix together the tomato purée, sherry and stock and add to the dish. Bring to the boil, then reduce the heat and cover with a lid.

5. Place in a preheated oven, 150°C (300°F), Gas Mark 2, for about 3½ hours or until the meat is meltingly tender and falling from the bone. Check the seasoning and serve with plenty of crusty bread.

Beef Goulash

———

SERVES 8 | PREPARATION TIME 10 minutes | COOKING TIME 2–2½ hours

4 tablespoons olive oil

1.5 kg (3 lb) braising steak, cubed

2 onions, sliced

2 red peppers, cored, deseeded and diced

1 tablespoon smoked paprika

2 tablespoons chopped marjoram

1 teaspoon caraway seeds

1 litre (1¾ pints) beef stock (see page 7)

5 tablespoons tomato purée

salt and pepper

1. Heat the oil in a flameproof casserole, add the beef, in 3 batches, and cook over a high heat for 5 minutes until browned all over. Remove from the pan with a slotted spoon.

2. Add the onions and red peppers to the pan and cook gently for 10 minutes until softened. Stir in the paprika, marjoram and caraway seeds and cook, stirring, for a further 1 minute.

3. Return the beef to the pan, add the stock, tomato purée and salt and pepper to taste and bring to the boil, stirring. Reduce the heat, cover and simmer gently for 1½–2 hours. You can remove the lid for the final 30 minutes if the sauce needs thickening.

Beef & Cabbage with Caraway Dumplings

SERVES 4 | PREPARATION TIME 20 minutes | COOKING TIME 1 hour 40 minutes

25 g (1 oz) butter

1 kg (2 lb) beef stewing steak, cut into 1.5 cm (¾ inch) cubes

1 large onion, thinly sliced

1 garlic clove, finely chopped

1 tablespoon paprika

½ teaspoon caraway seeds

1 cabbage, shredded

500 g (1 lb) tomatoes, skinned and roughly chopped

CARAWAY DUMPLINGS

250 g (8 oz) wholemeal flour

½ teaspoon salt

1 teaspoon bicarbonate of soda

1 teaspoon paprika

1 teaspoon caraway seeds

125 g (4 oz) shredded suet

200 ml (7 fl oz) water

2 tablespoons tomato purée

1. Melt half the butter in a flameproof casserole over a high heat. Add the beef cubes and brown well on all sides, turning occasionally. Remove the beef from the casserole with a slotted spoon.

2. Lower the heat and add the onion and garlic. Cook, stirring occasionally, until softened. Stir in the paprika, caraway seeds, cabbage and tomatoes. Pour in the stock and bring to the boil. Cover the casserole and transfer to a preheated oven, 180°C (350°F), Gas Mark 4, for 1 hour.

3. In the meantime, make the dumplings. Put the flour, salt, bicarbonate of soda, paprika, caraway seeds and suet into a mixing bowl. Mix the measurement water with the tomato purée, add to the flour mixture and mix well to make a dough. Divide the dough into 16 portions.

4. Put the dumplings on top of the beef and cabbage and cook, uncovered, for 20 minutes or until the dumplings are light and fluffy.

Creamy Pork & Cider Hotpot

SERVES 4 | PREPARATION TIME 25 minutes | COOKING TIME 1½ hours

2 teaspoons plain flour

625 g (1¼ lb) lean boneless leg of pork, trimmed of any excess fat and cut into bite-sized chunks

25 g (1 oz) butter

1 tablespoon olive oil

1 small onion, chopped

1 large leek, trimmed, cleaned and chopped

450 ml (¾ pint) cider

1 tablespoon chopped sage

2 tablespoons wholegrain mustard

2 pears

100 ml (3½ fl oz) crème fraîche

450 g (14½ oz) sweet potatoes, scrubbed and thinly sliced

2 tablespoons chilli oil

salt

chopped flat leaf parsley, to garnish

1. Season the flour with a little salt and use to coat the pieces of meat.

2. Melt the butter with the oil in a shallow flameproof casserole and gently fry the pork in batches until lightly browned. Remove each batch with a slotted spoon and set aside on a warm plate.

3. Add the onion and leek to the casserole, and fry gently for 5 minutes until soft and translucent. Return the meat to the pan, along with the cider, sage and mustard. Bring just to the boil, then cover, reduce the heat to as low as possible and simmer gently for 30 minutes.

4. Peel, core and thickly slice the pears. Stir the crème fraîche into the sauce, then scatter the pear slices on top. Arrange the sweet potato slices in overlapping layers on top, putting the end pieces underneath and keeping the best slices for the top layer. Brush with the chilli oil and sprinkle with salt.

5. Cook in a preheated oven, 160°C (325°F), Gas Mark 3, for 45 minutes or until the sweet potatoes are tender and lightly browned. Scatter with the chopped parsley and serve hot.

Catalan Pork Stew

SERVES 4 | PREPARATION TIME 20 minutes | COOKING TIME 1¼ hours

150 ml (¼ pint) olive oil

750 g (1½ lb) lean pork, cut into 2.5 cm (1 inch) cubes

1 large onion, peeled and sliced

2 garlic cloves, crushed

400 g (13 oz) can chopped tomatoes

1 green pepper, cored, deseeded and chopped

1½ teaspoons paprika

150 ml (¼ pint) chicken or vegetable stock (see page 7)

salt and pepper

chopped coriander, to garnish

1. Heat 2 tablespoons of the olive oil in a large heavy-based saucepan, add the pork and fry gently until golden brown on all sides, turning occasionally. Remove from the saucepan with a slotted spoon.

2. Add the onion and garlic to the cooking juices in the saucepan and cook until soft and golden. Return to the meat to the saucepan, and stir in the tomatoes, green pepper, paprika and stock. Season with salt and pepper. Bring to the boil, cover tightly and simmer gently for 1 hour or until the meat is tender.

3. Serve garnished with the chopped coriander and with plain boiled rice.

Pork, Leek & Apple Casserole

SERVES 4 | PREPARATION TIME 25 minutes | COOKING TIME 1½ hours

2 tablespoons olive oil

750 g (1½ lb) lean pork, cut into 1.5 cm (¾ inch) cubes

1 large green dessert apple, cored and sliced

1 large onion, thinly sliced

750 g (1½ lb) potatoes, diced

1 teaspoon mustard powder

300 ml (½ pint) chicken or vegetable stock (see page 7)

300 ml (½ pint) dry cider

750 g (1½ lb) leeks, cut into 1.5 cm (¾ inch) chunks

4 sage leaves, chopped

1. Heat the oil in large flameproof casserole over a high heat. Add the pork and fry until golden brown on all sides, turning occasionally. Remove the pork with a slotted spoon.

2. Lower the heat and add the apple and onion to the casserole and cook for 5 minutes, stirring occasionally. Add the potatoes, stirring to combine and scatter in the mustard powder. Cook, stirring, for 1 minute. Add the stock and cider and bring to the boil. Add the pork, leeks and sage, stir and cover.

3. Transfer to a preheated oven, 180°C (350°F), Gas Mark 4, for 1¼ hours, or until the meat is tender.

Lamb Hotpot with Dumplings

———

SERVES 4 | PREPARATION TIME 30 minutes | COOKING TIME about 1 hour

1 tablespoon vegetable oil

1 small onion, chopped

375 g (12 oz) boneless lamb, cubed

1 leek, chopped

75 g (3 oz) ready-to-eat dried apricots, chopped

375 g (12 oz) new potatoes, halved

1 tablespoon thyme leaves

2 tablespoons plain flour

600 ml (1 pint) lamb stock

DUMPLINGS

125 g (4 oz) plain flour

½ teaspoon salt

1 teaspoon thyme leaves

50 g (2 oz) vegetable suet

about 4 tablespoons cold water

1. Heat the oil in a large, heavy-based saucepan and cook the onion and lamb over a moderate heat for 4–5 minutes until golden and soft. Add the leek, apricots and new potatoes and cook for 2 minutes, then add the thyme and flour and stir well to coat lightly. Pour in the stock, then bring to the boil and cover and simmer gently for 35 minutes, stirring occasionally.

2. Meanwhile, make the dumplings. Place the flour and salt in a bowl with the thyme leaves and suet and mix well. Mix in enough water to make an elastic dough. Divide into 12 and shape into small walnut-sized balls using lightly floured hands. Stir the hotpot and top up with a little water if necessary, then drop the dumplings into the stock and cover and simmer for 15 minutes until the dumplings have almost doubled in size.

3. Serve the hotpot ladled into warm serving bowls with the dumplings.

Lamb & Lemon Cobbler

———

SERVES 4 | PREPARATION TIME 25 minutes | COOKING TIME 1 hour 40 minutes

2 tablespoons olive oil

750 g (1½ lb) lean lamb, cut into 1.5 cm (¾ inch) cubes

500 g (1 lb) white turnips, cut into 1.5 cm (¾ inch) cubes

1 large onion, chopped

375 g (12 oz) carrots, chopped

300 ml (½ pint) lamb stock

1 bay leaf

juice of ½ lemon

125 g (4 oz) watercress, chopped

COBBLER

250 g (8 oz) wholemeal flour

1 teaspoon mustard powder

1 teaspoon bicarbonate of soda

grated rind of 1 lemon

1 tablespoon chopped thyme

1 tablespoon chopped parsley

75 g (3 oz) butter

1 egg, beaten

75 ml (3 fl oz) milk

salt and pepper

1. Heat the oil in a large flameproof casserole over a medium heat. Add the lamb and fry until brown on all sides, turning occasionally. Remove with a slotted spoon.

2. Lower the heat and add the turnips and onion and cook uncovered, stirring occasionally, for 5 minutes. Add the carrots and stock and bring to the boil. Add the herbs and lemon juice, then cover the casserole and transfer to a preheated oven, 180°C (350°F), Gas Mark 4, for 1 hour.

3. Make the cobbler. Put the flour, pinch of salt, pepper, mustard powder, bicarbonate of soda, lemon rind and herbs in mixing bowl. Rub in the butter with your fingertips until it resembles fine breadcrumbs. Make a well in the centre, add the milk and egg and mix to a dough. Divide the dough and form into 8 scones.

4. Remove the casserole from the oven and mix in the watercress. Heat the oven to 200°C (400°F), Gas Mark 6. Place the scones of top of the lamb, return the casserole to the oven and cook for 20 minutes or until the scones are firm and beginning to brown. Serve immediately.

Irish Stew

———

SERVES 4–6 | PREPARATION TIME 25 minutes | COOKING TIME 1½ hours

750 g (1½ lb) lean lamb, cut into 1.5 cm (¾ inch) cubes
1 kg (2 lb) potatoes, cut into 1.5 cm (¾ inch) cubes
500 g (1 lb) carrots, diced
6 celery sticks, diced
2 large onions, peeled and thinly sliced
6 tablespoons chopped parsley
1.2 litres (2 pints) lamb stock
salt and pepper

1. Layer the meat, vegetables and parsley in a large flameproof casserole or saucepan, seasoning each layer well with pepper and lightly with salt.

2. Pour over the stock, topping up with a little water if the stock doesn't quite cover the layers of meat and vegetables.

3. Bring the stew to the boil over a medium heat, then cover and simmer for 1½ hours. Serve ladled into deep bowls with some of the cooking broth. Any leftover cooking broth can be used to make soup.

131

127

126

122

Pies, Rice
& Veg

Beef & Mustard Pies
Game Pie
Fish Pie
Chicken Picnic Terrine
Creamy Chicken Risotto
Baked Mushroom Risotto
Barley Risotto with Chicken
Mixed Bean Casserole
Pumpkin & Root Vegetable Stew
Roast Potatoes with Garlic & Tomatoes
Potatoes Dauphinoise
Pumpkin, Leek & Potato Bake
Braised Red Cabbage
Home Baked Beans

Beef & Mustard Pies

Makes 4 | PREPARATION TIME 30 minutes, plus cooling | COOKING TIME about 2½ hours

1 tablespoon sunflower oil

750 g (1½ lb) diced stewing steak, any fat discarded

4 smoked streaky bacon rashers, diced

1 onion, chopped

200 ml (7 fl oz) red wine

400 ml (14 fl oz) beef stock (see page 7)

1 tablespoon tomato purée

2 teaspoons mustard powder

6 bay leaves

1 tablespoon cornflour, mixed with a little water

25 g (1 oz) butter

250 g (8 oz) shallots, halved if large

325 g (11 oz) ready-made shortcrust pastry

beaten egg, to glaze

salt and pepper

1. Heat the oil in a frying pan and add the beef, a few pieces at a time, until it has all been added to the pan. Fry over a high heat, stirring until browned on all sides. Lift out of the pan and transfer to a casserole dish.

2. Fry the bacon and onion until golden, then add the wine, stock, tomato purée and mustard powder. Add 2 bay leaves and season generously with salt and pepper. Add the cornflour mix, bring to the boil, stirring until thickened, then pour over the beef.

3. Cover the casserole dish and cook in a preheated oven, 180°C (350°F), Gas Mark 4, for 2 hours until the beef is very tender. Heat the butter in a clean frying pan and fry the shallots until golden (about 5 minutes). Add to the beef casserole and leave to cool.

4. Divide the beef mixture between 4 × 300 ml (½ pint) individual ovenproof pie dishes. Cut the pastry into 4, then roll one piece out to make a pie lid. Brush the rim of a dish with beaten egg and lay the pastry over the dish. Press the pastry on to the dish edge. Trim off the excess pastry and fork the edge. Repeat until 4 pies have been made. Brush with egg, add a bay leaf to each for decoration, then bake in a preheated oven, 190°C (375°F), Gas Mark 5, for 20–25 minutes until the pastry is golden and the filling piping hot.

Game Pie

SERVES 4 | PREPARATION TIME 45 minutes, plus cooling | COOKING TIME 2 hours

25 g (1 oz) butter

1 tablespoon olive oil

1 oven-ready pheasant, halved

1 oven-ready pigeon, halved

2 rabbit or chicken leg joints

1 large onion, roughly
chopped

100 g (3½ oz) smoked streaky
bacon, diced

2 tablespoons plain flour

200 ml (7 fl oz) red wine

400 ml (13 fl oz) chicken stock
(see page 7)

2 tablespoons redcurrant jelly

1 teaspoon juniper or allspice
berries, roughly crushed

1 bouquet garni

375 g (12 oz) ready-made puff
pastry, defrosted if frozen

beaten egg, to glaze

salt and pepper

1. Heat the butter and oil in a large frying pan, then fry the game, in batches, until browned. Lift out and put into a large casserole dish. Add the onion and bacon to the frying pan and fry for 5 minutes, stirring until golden. Mix in the flour, then stir in the wine, stock and redcurrant jelly. Add the berries, bouquet garni and seasoning, then bring to the boil. Tip the sauce over the game, cover and cook in a preheated oven, 160°C (325°F), Gas Mark 3, for 1¼ hours. Leave to cool.

2. Lift out the game and take the meat off the bone. Return the meat to the sauce, discard the bouquet garni, then spoon into a 1.2 litre (2 pint) pie dish.

3. Roll out the pastry on a lightly floured surface until a little larger than the top of the pie dish. Cut 1 cm (½ inch) wide strips from the edges and stick on to the dish rim with beaten egg. Brush the pastry strips with egg and lay the sheet of pastry on top. Press down and trim off the excess pastry. Press your first and second fingers onto the pie edge, then make small cuts between them with a small knife to create a scalloped edge. Repeat all the way around the pie. Cut leaves from the rerolled trimmings and decorate.

4. Brush the pie with beaten egg, then cook in a preheated oven, 200°C (400°F), Gas Mark 6, for 30–35 minutes until golden and piping hot inside.

Fish Pie

300 g (10 oz) peeled and deveined raw prawns, thawed if frozen

2 teaspoons cornflour

300 g (10 oz) white fish fillets such as haddock, skinned and cut into small pieces

2 teaspoons green peppercorns in brine, rinsed and drained

1 small fennel bulb, roughly chopped

1 small leek, trimmed, cleaned and roughly chopped

15 g (½ oz) dill

15 g (½ oz) flat leaf parsley

100 g (3½ oz) fresh or frozen green peas

350 g (12 oz) ready-made cheese sauce

750 g (1½ lb) baking potatoes, thinly sliced

75 g (3 oz) Cheddar cheese, grated

salt and pepper

1. Dry the prawns, if frozen and thawed, by patting between sheets of kitchen paper. Season the cornflour with salt and pepper and use to coat the prawns and white fish. Lightly crush the peppercorns using a mortar and pestle.

2. Put the peppercorns in a food processor with the fennel, leek, dill, parsley and a little salt and blend until very finely chopped, scraping the mixture down from the sides of the bowl if necessary. Tip into a shallow ovenproof dish. Scatter the prawns and fish over the fennel mixture, and mix together a little. Scatter the peas on top.

3. Spoon half the cheese sauce over the filling, and spread roughly with the back of a spoon. Layer the potatoes on top, overlapping the slices and seasoning each layer with salt and pepper as you go. Spoon the remaining sauce over the top, spreading it in a thin layer. Sprinkle with the cheese.

4. Bake in a preheated oven, 220°C (425°F), Gas Mark 7, for 30 minutes until the surface has turned pale golden. Reduce the oven temperature to 180°C (350°F), Gas Mark 4, and cook for a further 30–40 minutes until the potatoes are completely tender and the fish is cooked through.

Chicken Picnic Terrine

———

SERVES 8 | PREPARATION TIME 40 minutes, plus chilling | COOKING TIME 1 hour 35 minutes

300 g (10 oz) smoked streaky bacon

1 tablespoon olive oil

1 onion, finely chopped

8 Toulouse sausages, about 600 g (1 lb 2 oz), skins removed

125 g (4 oz) chicken livers, defrosted if frozen, diced

4 boneless, skinless chicken thighs, cut into small dice

1 Granny Smith dessert apple, cored and coarsely grated

¼ teaspoon grated nutmeg

50 g (2 oz) whole pistachio nuts

50 g (2 oz) fresh breadcrumbs

4 tablespoons dry sherry or brandy

salt and pepper

1. Use a strip of non-stick baking paper to line the base and short sides of a 1 kg (2 lb) loaf tin. Stretch each bacon rasher so it is half as long again, then butt close together to line the tin. Cut rashers in half to line the ends of the tin, and set aside a few rashers.

2. Heat the oil in a frying pan, add the onion and fry for 5 minutes until softened.

3. Mix the sausage meat, chicken livers, chicken thighs, apple, nutmeg, nuts, breadcrumbs and sherry or brandy in a large bowl, then stir in the onions and seasoning. Spoon the mixture into the bacon-lined tin, pressing it down well. Fold the ends of the bacon over the top, then cover the gaps with the reserved rashers. Cover with foil, stand the tin in a roasting tin and pour in hot water to come halfway up the sides. Cook in a preheated oven, 180°C (350°F), Gas Mark 4, for 1½ hours.

4. Tip the water out of the roasting tin. Cool the terrine then cover top of the loaf tin with weights and chill overnight. Loosen the edges of the terrine, turn it out of the tin and peel away the lining paper. Cut into thick slices and serve.

Creamy Chicken Risotto

SERVES 6 | PREPARATION TIME 35 minutes | COOKING TIME 2 hours

1 kg (2 lb) whole chicken

2 litres (3½ pints) water

2 celery sticks

2 onions

2 carrots

3–4 tablespoons olive oil

7 tablespoons white wine

375 g (12 oz) tomatoes, skinned and mashed

500 g (1 lb) risotto rice

75 g (3 oz) butter, softened

75 g (3 oz) Parmesan cheese, freshly grated

1–2 tablespoons chopped parsley, to garnish

salt and pepper

1. Remove the bones from the chicken and place them in a large pan with the water. Add 1 celery stick, 1 onion, 1 carrot and seasoning. Cover and simmer for 1½ hours. Strain the stock and keep hot.

2. Meanwhile, dice the chicken meat, discarding all the skin. Finely chop the remaining celery, onion and carrot. Heat the oil, add the chopped vegetables and sauté until lightly coloured. Add the chicken and cook, stirring for 5 minutes. Add the wine and cook, stirring, until it has evaporated.

3. Add the tomatoes and season to taste. Cover and cook over a low heat for 20 minutes, adding a little of the hot chicken stock if the mixture becomes dry.

4. Add the rice, then add the hot stock, a large ladleful at a time, stirring until each addition is absorbed into the rice. Continue adding stock in this way, cooking for 20 minutes until the rice is creamy.

5. Remove from the heat, add the butter and Parmesan and fold in gently. Cover and leave the risotto to rest for a few minutes before serving, sprinkled with parsley.

Baked Mushroom Risotto

―――

SERVES 4 | PREPARATION TIME 15 minutes, plus soaking | COOKING TIME 1¼ hours

30 g (1½ oz) dried porcini
   mushrooms, soaked in
   125 ml (4 fl oz) boiling water
   for 10–15 minutes

25 g (1 oz) butter

1 tablespoon olive oil

2 shallots, finely chopped

1 leek, trimmed, cleaned and
   finely chopped

1 large garlic clove, finely
   chopped

350 g (11½ oz) short-grain
   brown rice

50 ml (2 fl oz) Marsala

1.2 litres (2 pints) vegetable
   stock (see page 7)

125 g (4 oz) asparagus tips,
   chopped

salt and pepper

finely grated Parmesan
   cheese, to serve (optional)

1. Drain the porcini, reserving the soaking liquid, then squeeze dry and roughly chop.

2. Heat the butter and oil in a large, flameproof casserole over a low heat, add the shallots and leek and fry gently for 8 minutes or until softened. Add the garlic and fry for a further 2 minutes. Stir the rice into the pan and cook for 1–2 minutes, then pour over the Marsala and bubble, stirring continuously, until evaporated.

3. Mix in the mushrooms, reserved soaking liquid and stock, stir well and bring to the boil. Season to taste with salt and pepper, cover and place in a preheated oven, 180°C (350°F), Gas Mark 4, for 45 minutes, stirring occasionally.

4. Add the asparagus and stir well. Return to the oven for a further 15 minutes or until the rice is tender and most of the liquid has been absorbed. Remove from the oven and leave to stand for 2–3 minutes. Spoon the risotto into serving bowls and sprinkle with the grated Parmesan, if liked.

Barley Risotto with Chicken

———

SERVES 4 | PREPARATION TIME 15 minutes | COOKING TIME 1 hour 10 minutes

2 tablespoons olive oil

6 boneless, skinless chicken
thighs, diced

1 onion, roughly chopped

2 garlic cloves, finely chopped

200 g (7 oz) chestnut
mushrooms, sliced

250 g (8 oz) pearl barley

200 ml (7 fl oz) red wine

1.2 litres (2 pints) chicken
stock (see page 7)

salt and pepper

TO GARNISH

parsley, chopped

shavings of Parmesan cheese

1. Heat the oil in a large frying pan, add the chicken and onion and fry for 5 minutes, stirring until lightly browned.

2. Stir in the garlic and mushrooms and fry for 2 minutes, then mix in the barley. Add the red wine, half the stock and plenty of seasoning, then bring to the boil, stirring. Cover and simmer for 1 hour, topping up with extra stock as needed until the barley is soft.

3. Spoon into shallow bowls and garnish with the parsley and Parmesan.

Mixed Bean Casserole

———

SERVES 4 | PREPARATION TIME 20 minutes, plus soaking and standing | COOKING TIME 2 hours

500 g (1 lb) aubergines
1 tablespoon salt
4 tablespoons olive oil
1 garlic clove, finely chopped
2 onions, thinly sliced
500 g (1 lb) courgettes, thinly sliced
500 g (1 lb) tomatoes, chopped
250 g (8 oz) brown rice
75 g (3 oz) red kidney beans, soaked overnight, drained and rinsed
75 g (3 oz) black turtle beans, soaked overnight, drained and rinsed
75 g (3 oz) pinto beans, soaked overnight, drained and rinsed
600 ml (1 pint) vegetable stock (see page 7)
300 ml (½ pint) tomato juice
50 g (2 oz) mature Cheddar cheese
25 g (1 oz) dried breadcrumbs

1. Dice the aubergines, place in a colander and sprinkle with the salt. Leave to drain for 20 minutes, then rinse under cold water and pat dry with kitchen towel.

2. Heat the oil in a large flameproof casserole over a low heat. Add the garlic and onion and fry gently for 5 minutes, stirring occasionally. Add the courgettes, tomatoes, rice, beans, aubergines and mix. Add the stock and tomato juice and bring to the boil.

3. Cover the casserole and transfer to a preheated oven, 180°C (350°F), Gas Mark 4, for 1½ hours, or until the beans are soft and most of the liquid has been absorbed.

4. Mix the Cheddar and breadcrumbs together, scatter evenly across the top of the casserole, return to oven and cook, uncovered, for 15 minutes, or until the cheese melts and begins to brown. Serve immediately.

Pumpkin & Root Vegetable Stew

———

SERVES 8–10 | PREPARATION TIME 20 minutes | COOKING TIME 1½–2 hours

1 pumpkin, about 1.5 kg (3 lb)

4 tablespoons sunflower or
  olive oil

1 large onion, finely chopped

3–4 garlic cloves, finely
  chopped

1 small red chilli, deseeded
  and chopped

4 celery sticks, cut into 2.5 cm
  (1 inch) lengths

500 g (1 lb) carrots, cut into
  2.5 cm (1 inch) pieces

250 g (8 oz) parsnips, cut into
  2.5 cm (1 inch) pieces

2 x 400g (13 oz) cans plum
  tomatoes

3 tablespoons tomato purée

1–2 tablespoons hot paprika

250 ml (8 fl oz) vegetable stock
  (see page 7)

1 bouquet garni

2 x 400 g (13 oz) cans red
  kidney beans, drained

salt and pepper

3–4 tablespoons finely
  chopped parsley, to garnish

1. Slice the pumpkin in half and discard the seeds and fibres. Cut the flesh into cubes, removing the skin. You should have about 1 kg (2 lb) pumpkin flesh.

2. Heat the oil in a large saucepan over a medium heat, add the onion, garlic and chilli and fry until softened but not coloured. Add the pumpkin and celery and fry gently for 10 minutes.

3. Stir in the carrots, parsnips, tomatoes, tomato purée, paprika, stock and bouquet garni. Bring to the boil, then reduce the heat, cover the pan and simmer for 1–1½ hours or until the vegetables are almost tender.

4. Add the beans and cook for 10 minutes. Season with salt and pepper and sprinkle with the parsley. Serve with crusty bread or garlic mashed potatoes.

Roast Potatoes with Garlic & Tomatoes

SERVES 4 | PREPARATION TIME 10 minutes | COOKING TIME 1 hour

625 g (1¼ lb) potatoes, unpeeled

2 onions, thickly sliced

1 garlic bulb, broken into cloves

200 g (7 oz) cherry tomatoes, on the vine

3 tablespoons olive oil

150 ml (¼ pint) dry white wine

1 teaspoon dried oregano

pared rind of 1 small orange

salt and pepper

1. Cut the potatoes in half lengthways, then each half into 3 wedges. Put in a large roasting tin with all the remaining ingredients, season with salt and pepper and stir well to combine thoroughly.

2. Roast in a preheated oven, 200°C (400°F), Gas Mark 6, for 1 hour, or until the potatoes are cooked through. Stir the vegetables in the tin a couple of times during cooking. If the liquid dries out so much that the tomatoes and onions begin to stick to the base, add a little hot water to stop them burning.

Potatoes Dauphinoise

———

SERVES 4–6 | PREPARATION TIME 10 minutes | COOKING TIME 1–1¼ hours

750 g–1 kg (1½–2 lb) evenly
   shaped potatoes, peeled
   and thinly sliced
1 teaspoon grated nutmeg
1 garlic clove, crushed
300 ml (½ pint) double cream
75 g (3 oz) Gruyère or
   Cheddar cheese, grated
salt and pepper

1. Arrange the potatoes in layers in a well-greased ovenproof dish, sprinkling each layer with nutmeg, salt and pepper.

2. Stir the crushed garlic clove into the cream and pour the cream over the potatoes. Sprinkle the cheese over the surface so that the potatoes are completely covered. Cover with foil and bake in a preheated oven, 180°C (350°F), Gas Mark 4, for 45 minutes.

3. Remove the foil and cook for 15–30 minutes more, or until the potatoes are cooked through and the cheese topping is crusty and golden brown.

Pumpkin, Leek & Potato Bake

SERVES 4 | PREPARATION TIME 30 minutes | COOKING TIME 2 hours

4 tablespoons hot horseradish
   sauce
1 tablespoon chopped thyme
300 ml (½ pint) double cream
1 large leek, finely shredded
100 g (3½ oz) walnuts, roughly
   chopped
500 g (1 lb) pumpkin
750 g (1½ lb) baking potatoes,
   thinly sliced
150 ml (¼ pint) vegetable
   stock (see page 7)
50 g (2 oz) breadcrumbs
40 g (1½ oz) butter, melted
2 tablespoons pumpkin seeds
salt

1. Mix the horseradish sauce in a large bowl with the thyme and half the cream. Add the leek and all but 2 tablespoons of the walnuts and mix well.

2. Cut the pumpkin into chunks, discarding the skin and seeds. Thinly slice the chunks.

3. Scatter half the potatoes in a 2 litre (3½ pint) shallow, ovenproof dish, seasoning lightly with salt, and cover with half the pumpkin chunks. Spoon the leek mixture on top, spreading in an even layer. Arrange the remaining pumpkin slices on top and then the remaining potato slices. Sprinkle with salt.

4. Mix the remaining cream with the stock and pour over the potatoes. Mix the breadcrumbs with the butter and sprinkle over the top. Scatter with the pumpkin seeds and remaining nuts. Cover with foil and bake in a preheated oven, 180°C (350°F), Gas Mark 4, for 1 hour. Remove the foil and bake for a further 45–60 minutes until golden and the vegetables feel tender when pierced with a knife.

Braised Red Cabbage

SERVES 8 | PREPARATION TIME 15 minutes | COOKING TIME 2¼ hours

1 head red cabbage, about
   1.5 kg (3 lb), finely shredded

50 g (2 oz) butter

2 Spanish onions, thinly sliced

4 tablespoons brown sugar

250 g (8 oz) tart dessert
   apples, peeled, cored and
   chopped

150 ml (¼ pint) vegetable
   stock (see page 7)

150 ml (¼ pint) red wine

3 tablespoons wine vinegar
   or cider vinegar

1 small raw beetroot, coarsely
   grated

salt and pepper

1. Put the cabbage in a large bowl. Cover with boiling water and set aside.

2. Using a large heavy-based pan, melt the butter. Add the onions and fry, stirring frequently, over a moderate heat until soft and transparent. Stir in the sugar and continue to fry gently until the onions are caramelized and a rich golden colour. Take great care not to let the sugar burn.

3. Drain the cabbage thoroughly. Add it to the pan with the apples, stock, wine and vinegar. Mix well. Season generously with salt and pepper. Cover tightly and cook gently for 1½ hours, stirring occasionally. Mix in the grated beetroot and continue to cook, covered, for 30 minutes longer, or until the cabbage is soft. Adjust the seasoning, if necessary, and serve very hot.

Home Baked Beans

SERVES 4–6 | PREPARATION TIME 10 minutes | COOKING TIME about 2 hours

2 x 400 g (13 oz) cans borlotti beans, drained

1 garlic clove, crushed

1 onion, finely chopped

450 ml (¾ pint) vegetable stock (see page 7)

300 ml (½ pint) passata (sieved tomatoes)

2 tablespoons molasses or black treacle

2 tablespoons tomato purée

2 tablespoons soft dark brown sugar

1 tablespoon Dijon mustard

1 tablespoon red wine vinegar

salt and pepper

1. Put all the ingredients in a flameproof casserole with a little salt and pepper. Cover and bring slowly to the boil.

2. Bake in a preheated oven, 160°C (325°F), Gas Mark 3, for 1½ hours. Remove the lid and bake for a further 30 minutes until the sauce is syrupy. Serve with hot buttered toast.

137

151

146

141

Slow Cooker Classics

———

Old English Pea & Ham Soup
Carrot & Ginger Soup
Lamb & Barley Broth
Leek, Potato & Stilton Soup
Cock-a-Leekie Soup
Creamy Tarragon Chicken
Sweet & Sour Chicken
Pot-roast Pheasant with Chestnuts
Braised Duck with Orange Sauce
Venison Sausage & Lentil Stew
Turkey & Sausage Stew
Cassoulet
Smoked Mackerel Kedgeree
Bacon & Leek Suet Pudding
Potato, Apple & Bacon Hotpot
Cidered Pork with Sage Dumplings
Honey-glazed Gammon
Beef & Root Vegetable Hotpot
Beef & Guinness Puff Pies
Sausages with Onion Gravy
Lamb Hotchpotch
Slow-cooked Lamb Shanks
Mushroom & Chestnut Pudding

Old English Pea & Ham Soup

SERVES 4–6 | PREPARATION TIME 15 minutes, plus soaking | COOKING TEMPERATURE high | COOKING TIME 5–6 hours

175 g (6 oz) dried green split peas, soaked overnight in cold water

2 onions, chopped

2 celery sticks, diced

1 carrot, diced

1.5 litres (2½ pints) water

3 teaspoons English mustard

1 bay leaf

1 small unsmoked boneless bacon joint, about 500 g (1 lb)

4 tablespoons chopped parsley

salt and pepper

1. Preheat the slow cooker if necessary. Drain the peas and add to a large saucepan with the onions, celery, carrot and water. Bring to the boil, skim if needed and boil for 10 minutes.

2. Pour the mixture into the slow cooker pot, then stir in the mustard, bay leaf and some pepper. Rinse the bacon joint in several changes of cold water, then add to the pot and press below the surface of the liquid. Cover and cook on high for 5–6 hours or until the peas are soft and the bacon cooked through.

3. Lift the bacon joint out of the slow cooker pot with a carving fork, drain well, then cut away the rind and fat. Cut the meat into bite-sized pieces. Purée the soup with a stick blender or leave chunky, if preferred. Stir the bacon back into the pot and mix in the parsley. Taste and adjust the seasoning, adding salt, if needed. Ladle the soup into bowls and serve with crusty bread.

Carrot & Ginger Soup

———

SERVES 6 | PREPARATION TIME 30 minutes | COOKING TEMPERATURE low | COOKING TIME 4¼–5¼ hours

1 tablespoon sunflower oil
15 g (½ oz) butter
1 large onion, finely chopped
500 g (1 lb) carrots, diced
75 g (3 oz) red lentils
3.5 cm (1½ inch) piece fresh
   root ginger, peeled and
   finely chopped
3 teaspoons mild curry paste
1.2 litres (2 pints) hot chicken
   or vegetable stock (see
   page 7)
300 ml (½ pint) full-fat milk
salt and pepper
coriander sprigs, to garnish

1. Preheat the slow cooker if necessary. Heat the oil and butter in a frying pan, Add the onion and fry, stirring, for 5 minutes until pale golden.

2. Transfer the onion to the slow cooker pot and add the carrots, lentils and ginger. Mix the curry paste into the hot stock, pour into the pot and season well with salt and pepper. Stir together then cover with the lid and cook on low for 4–5 hours.

3. The soup can be left chunky at this stage or puréed in a food processor or blender, in batches, until smooth. Stir in the milk, cook for 15 minutes until heated through, then ladle into bowls and garnish with coriander.

Lamb & Barley Broth

———

SERVES 4–6 | PREPARATION TIME 15 minutes | COOKING TEMPERATURE low | COOKING TIME 8–10 hours

25 g (1 oz) butter

1 tablespoon sunflower oil

1 lamb rump chop or 125 g (4 oz) lamb fillet, diced

1 onion, chopped

1 small leek, chopped

500 g (1 lb) mixed parsnip, swede, turnip and carrot, cut into small dice

50 g (2 oz) pearl barley

1.2 litres (2 pints) lamb stock or chicken stock (see page 7)

¼ teaspoon ground allspice

2–3 sprigs of rosemary

salt and pepper

chopped parsley or chives, to garnish (optional)

1. Preheat the slow cooker if necessary. Heat the butter and oil in a large frying pan, add the lamb, onion and leek and fry, stirring, until the lamb is lightly browned.

2. Stir in the root vegetables and barley, then add the stock, allspice, rosemary and plenty of salt and pepper and bring to the boil, stirring. Pour into the slow cooker pot, cover with the lid and cook on low for 8–10 hours or until the barley is tender. Stir well, taste and adjust the seasoning, if needed, then ladle the soup into bowls. Garnish with chopped herbs, if liked, and serve with warm bread.

Leek, Potato & Stilton Soup

———

SERVES 4–6 | PREPARATION TIME 25 minutes | COOKING TEMPERATURE low | COOKING TIME 5½–6½ hours

25 g (1 oz) butter

1 tablespoon sunflower oil

500 g (1 lb) leeks, thinly sliced; white and green parts kept separate

1 smoked back bacon rasher, diced, plus 4 grilled rashers, chopped, to garnish

375 g (12 oz) potatoes, diced

900 ml (1½ pints) chicken or vegetable stock (see page 7)

300 ml (½ pint) milk

150 ml (¼ pint) double cream

150 g (5 oz) mature Stilton (rind removed), diced

salt and pepper

1. Preheat the slow cooker if necessary. Heat the butter and oil in a large frying pan, then add the white leeks, the diced bacon and potatoes and fry over a medium heat, stirring, until just beginning to turn golden.

2. Pour in the stock, add a little salt and pepper and bring to the boil, stirring. Transfer to the slow cooker pot, cover with the lid and cook on low for 5–6 hours. Stir the reserved green leek slices and milk into the slow cooker pot. Replace the lid and cook, still on low, for 30 minutes or until the leeks are tender. Roughly purée the soup in the pot with a stick blender or use a masher, if preferred.

3. Mix in the cream and two-thirds of the cheese and stir until the cheese has melted. Taste and adjust the seasoning, if needed, then ladle the soup into bowls and sprinkle with the remaining cheese and chopped grilled bacon.

Cock-a-Leekie Soup

———

SERVES 6 | PREPARATION TIME 35 minutes | COOKING TEMPERATURE low | COOKING TIME 4¼–6¼ hours

2 leeks, about 500 g (1 lb),
    trimmed and cleaned

25 g (1 oz) butter

1 tablespoon sunflower oil

4 boneless, skinless chicken
    thighs, diced

1 potato, about 250 g (8 oz),
    diced

1 litre (1¾ pints) hot chicken
    stock (see page 7)

65 g (2½ oz) pitted prunes

salt and pepper

1. Preheat the slow cooker if necessary. Thinly slice the leeks and separate the green slices from the white.

2. Heat the butter and oil in a frying pan, add the diced chicken and fry for 5 minutes, stirring, until browned. Add the white sliced leek and potato and fry for 2 more minutes.

3. Transfer the chicken and leek mixture to the slow cooker pot. Pour in the stock, then stir in the prunes and a little salt and pepper. Cover with the lid and cook on low for 4–6 hours. When almost ready to serve, stir in the reserved sliced green leek into the soup and cook for 15 minutes.

Creamy Tarragon Chicken

———

SERVES 4 | PREPARATION TIME 15 minutes | COOKING TEMPERATURE high | COOKING TIME 3-4 hours

1 tablespoon olive oil

15 g (½ oz) butter

4 boneless, skinless chicken
   breasts, about 650 g
   (1 lb 6 oz) in total

200 g (7 oz) shallots, halved

1 tablespoon plain flour

300 ml (½ pint) chicken stock
   (see page 7)

4 tablespoons dry vermouth

2 sprigs of tarragon, plus extra
   to serve

3 tablespoons double cream

2 tablespoons chopped chives

salt and pepper

1. Preheat the slow cooker if necessary. Heat the oil and butter in a frying pan, add the chicken and fry over a high heat until golden on both sides but not cooked through. Drain and put into the slow cooker pot in a single layer.

2. Add the shallots to the frying pan and cook, stirring, for 4-5 minutes or until just beginning to turn golden. Stir in the flour, then gradually mix in the stock and vermouth. Add the sprigs of tarragon, a little salt and pepper and bring to the boil, stirring. Pour the sauce over the chicken breasts, cover with the lid and cook on high for 3-4 hours or until the chicken is cooked through to the centre.

3. Stir the cream into the sauce and sprinkle the chicken with 1 tablespoon chopped tarragon and the chives. Serve with coarsely mashed potatoes mixed with peas.

Sweet & Sour Chicken

SERVES 4 | PREPARATION TIME 20 minutes | COOKING TEMPERATURE low | COOKING TIME 6¼–8¼ hours

1 tablespoon sunflower oil

8 small chicken thighs, about 1 kg (2 lb) in total, skinned, boned and cubed

4 spring onions, thickly sliced; white and green parts kept separate

2 carrots, halved lengthways and thinly sliced

2.5 cm (1 inch) fresh root ginger, peeled and finely chopped

430 g (14¼ oz) can pineapple chunks in natural juice

300 ml (½ pint) chicken stock (see page 7)

1 tablespoon cornflour

1 tablespoon tomato purée

2 tablespoons caster sugar

2 tablespoons soy sauce

2 tablespoons malt vinegar

225 g (7½ oz) can bamboo shoots, drained

125 g (4 oz) bean sprouts

100 g (3½ oz) mangetout, thinly sliced

1. Preheat the slow cooker if necessary. Heat the oil in a frying pan, add the chicken thighs and fry, stirring, until browned on all sides. Mix in the white sliced spring onions, carrots and ginger and cook for 2 minutes.

2. Stir in the pineapple chunks and their juice and the stock. Put the cornflour, tomato purée and sugar into a small bowl, then gradually mix in the soy sauce and vinegar to make a smooth paste. Stir into the frying pan and bring to the boil, stirring.

3. Tip the chicken and sauce into the slow cooker pot, add the bamboo shoots and press the chicken beneath the surface of the sauce. Cover with the lid and cook on low for 6–8 hours.

4. When almost ready to serve, add the green spring onion, the beansprouts and mangetout to the slow cooker pot and mix well. Replace the lid and cook, still on low, for 15 minutes or until the vegetables are just tender. Serve with rice.

Pot-roast Pheasant with Chestnuts

———

SERVES 2–3 | PREPARATION TIME 15 minutes | COOKING TEMPERATURE high | COOKING TIME 3–4 hours

1 oven-ready pheasant, about
   750 g (1½ lb)
25 g (1 oz) butter
1 tablespoon olive oil
200 g (7 oz) shallots, halved
50 g (2 oz) smoked streaky
   bacon, diced, or ready-
   diced pancetta
2 celery sticks, thickly sliced
1 tablespoon plain flour
300 ml (½ pint) chicken stock
   (see page 7)
4 tablespoons dry sherry
100 g (3½ oz) vacuum-packed
   prepared chestnuts
2–3 sprigs of thyme
salt and pepper

1. Preheat the slow cooker if necessary. Rinse the pheasant inside and out with plenty of cold running water, then pat dry with kitchen towel.

2. Heat the butter and oil in a frying pan, add the pheasant, breast side down, the shallots, bacon or pancetta and celery and fry until golden brown, turning the pheasant and stirring the other ingredients. Transfer the pheasant to the slow cooker pot, placing it breast side down.

3. Stir the flour into the onion mix. Gradually add the stock and sherry, then add the chestnuts, thyme and a little salt and pepper. Bring to the boil, stirring, then spoon over the pheasant. Cover with the lid and cook on high for 3–4 hours until tender. Test with a knife through the thickest part of the pheasant leg and breast to make sure that the juices run clear. Carve the pheasant breast into thick slices and cut the legs away from the body. Serve with potatoes dauphinoise (see page 127).

Braised Duck with Orange Sauce

———

SERVES 4 | PREPARATION TIME 15 minutes | COOKING TEMPERATURE high | COOKING TIME 4–5 hours

4 duck legs, about 175 g
(6 oz) each

1 onion, sliced

2 tablespoons plain flour

150 ml (¼ pint) chicken stock
(see page 7)

150 ml (¼ pint) dry white wine

1 large orange, half sliced, half
squeezed juice

1 bay leaf

1 teaspoon Dijon mustard

salt

½ teaspoon black peppercorns,
roughly crushed

1. Preheat the slow cooker if necessary. Dry-fry the duck in a large frying pan over a low heat until the fat begins to run, then increase the heat until the duck is browned on both sides. Lift out of the pan with a slotted spoon and transfer to the slow cooker pot.

2. Pour off any excess fat to leave about 1 tablespoon. Fry the onions until softened. Stir in the flour, then mix in the stock, wine, orange juice, bay leaf, a little salt and the crushed peppercorns. Bring to the boil, stirring; add the sliced orange.

3. Pour the sauce over the duck, cover with the lid and cook on high for 4–5 hours or until the duck is tender and almost falling off the bones. Serve with rice and green beans.

Venison Sausage & Lentil Stew

———

SERVES 4 | PREPARATION TIME 20 minutes | COOKING TEMPERATURE low | COOKING TIME 6–7 hours

1 tablespoon olive oil

8 venison sausages

1 large onion, chopped

2 garlic cloves, chopped

2 tablespoons plain flour

900 ml (1½ pints) chicken stock (see page 7)

3 tablespoons brown sugar

2 tablespoons tomato purée

2 tablespoons balsamic vinegar

200 g (7 oz) puy lentils

250 g (8 oz) cranberries, thawed if frozen

2 bay leaves

salt and pepper

1. Preheat the slow cooker if necessary. Heat the oil in a frying pan, add the sausages and fry over a high heat until browned, but not cooked through. Transfer to a plate.

2. Add the onion to the pan and fry, stirring, until lightly browned. Add the garlic, then the flour. Stir in the stock, sugar, tomato purée and vinegar, season and bring to the boil.

3. Put the lentils, cranberries and bay leaves in the slow cooker pot, pour over the hot stock mixture then add the sausages. Cover with the lid and cook on low for 6–7 hours. Stir well, then spoon into shallow dishes to serve, discarding the bay leaves.

Turkey & Sausage Stew

_____

SERVES 4 | PREPARATION TIME 30 minutes | COOKING TEMPERATURE high | COOKING TIME 5½–6¾ hours

1 turkey drumstick, about
  700 g (1 lb 6 oz)

2 tablespoons sunflower oil

4 smoked streaky bacon
  rashers, diced

3 large pork & herb sausages,
  about 200 g (7 oz) in total,
  each cut into 4 pieces

1 onion, sliced

1 leek, sliced; white and green
  parts kept separate

2 tablespoons plain flour

600 ml (1 pint) chicken stock
  (see page 7)

small bunch of mixed herbs

300 g (10 oz) baby carrots,
  halved if large

2 celery sticks, sliced

65 g (2½ oz) fresh cranberries

salt and pepper

PARSLEY DUMPLINGS

150 g (5 oz) self-raising flour

75 g (3 oz) shredded suet

4 tablespoons chopped
  parsley

5–7 tablespoons water

1. Preheat the slow cooker if necessary. If the turkey drumstick does not fit into the slow cooker pot sever the knuckle end with a large heavy knife, hitting it with a rolling pin.

2. Heat the oil in a large frying pan, add the drumstick, bacon and sausage pieces and fry, turning until browned all over. Transfer to the slow cooker pot. Add the onion and white leeks slices to the pan and fry until softened. Stir in the flour, then mix in the stock. Add the herbs, salt and pepper and bring to the boil.

3. Add the carrots, celery and cranberries to the pot and pour over the hot onion mixture. Cover with the lid and cook on high for 5–6 hours or until the turkey is almost falling off the bone. Lift the turkey out of the slow cooker pot. Remove and discard the skin, then cut the meat into pieces, discarding the bones and tendons. Return meat to the pot with the reserved green leek slices.

4. To make the dumplings, mix the flour, suet, parsley and salt and pepper together in a bowl. Stir in enough water to make a soft dough. Knead, then shape into 12 small balls. Arrange over the turkey, replace the lid and cook, still on high, for 30–45 minutes or until the dumplings are cooked through. Spoon into shallow bowls to serve.

Cassoulet

SERVES 4 | PREPARATION TIME 30 minutes | COOKING TEMPERATURE low | COOKING TIME 8–9 hours

4 small duck legs

250 g (8 oz) lean pork belly
   rashers, rind removed, diced

1 large onion, chopped

2–3 garlic cloves, chopped

2 tablespoons plain flour

400 g (13 oz) can chopped
   tomatoes

200 ml (7 fl oz) red wine

100 ml (3½ fl oz) chicken stock
   (see page 7)

1 tablespoon brown sugar

2 teaspoons Dijon mustard

2 x 410 g (13½ oz) cans mixed
   beans, drained and rinsed

125 g (4 oz) piece chorizo
   sausage, diced

1 bouquet garni

40 g (1½ oz) fresh
   breadcrumbs

salt and pepper

1. Preheat the slow cooker if necessary. Dry-fry the duck legs in a frying pan until browned all over. Transfer to a plate. Pour all but 1 tablespoon duck fat from the pan.

2. Add the diced pork and onion to the pan and fry for 5 minutes, stirring, until lightly browned. Stir in the garlic and flour. Add the canned tomatoes, wine, stock, sugar and mustard. Season and bring to the boil, stirring.

3. Pour half the drained beans into the slow cooker pot. Arrange the duck pieces, chorizo and bouquet garni on top. Add the remaining beans, then pour in the pork and tomato mixture. Sprinkle with the breadcrumbs then cover with the lid and cook on low for 8–9 hours. Serve with a green salad.

Smoked Mackerel Kedgeree

———

SERVES 4 | PREPARATION TIME 15 minutes | COOKING TEMPERATURE low | COOKING TIME 3¼–4¼ hours

1 tablespoon sunflower oil

1 onion, chopped

1 teaspoon turmeric

2 tablespoons mango chutney

750–900 ml (1¼–1½ pints) vegetable stock (see page 7)

1 bay leaf

175 g (6 oz) easy-cook brown rice

250 g (8 oz) or 3 smoked mackerel fillets, skinned

100 g (3½ oz) frozen peas

25 g (1 oz) watercress or rocket leaves

4 hard-boiled eggs, cut into wedges, to garnish

salt and pepper

1. Preheat the slow cooker if necessary. Heat the oil in a frying pan, add the onion and fry, stirring, for 5 minutes or until softened and just beginning to turn golden.

2. Stir in the turmeric, chutney, stock, bay leaf and a little salt and pepper and bring to the boil. Pour into the slow cooker pot and add the rice. Add the smoked mackerel to the pot in a single layer. Cover with the lid and cook on low for 3–4 hours or until the rice is tender and has absorbed almost all the stock.

3. Stir in the peas, breaking up the fish into chunky pieces. Add extra hot stock if needed. Cook for 15 minutes more. Stir in the watercress or rocket, spoon on to plates and garnish with wedges of egg.

Bacon & Leek Suet Pudding

———

SERVES 4 | PREPARATION TIME 30 minutes | COOKING TEMPERATURE high | COOKING TIME 4–5 hours

25 g (1 oz) butter

2 smoked gammon steaks, about 450 g (14½ oz) in total, diced and any fat and rind discarded

250 g (8 oz) leeks, trimmed, cleaned and sliced

300 g (10 oz) self-raising flour

150 g (5 oz) vegetable suet

3 teaspoons dry mustard powder

200–250 ml (7–8 fl oz) water

salt and pepper

PARSLEY SAUCE

25 g (1 oz) butter

25 g (1 oz) plain flour

300 ml (½ pint) milk

20 g (¾ oz) parsley, finely chopped

1. Preheat the slow cooker if necessary. Heat the butter in a frying pan, add the gammon and leeks and fry, stirring, for 4–5 minutes or until the leeks have just softened. Season with pepper only. Leave to cool slightly.

2. Put the flour, ½ teaspoon salt, a large pinch of pepper, the suet and mustard powder in a bowl and mix well. Gradually stir in enough water to make a soft but not sticky dough. Knead lightly. Roll out on a large piece of floured nonstick baking paper to a rectangle 23 x 30 cm (9 x 12 inches). Turn the paper so that the shorter edges are facing you.

3. Spoon the gammon mixture over the pastry, leaving 2 cm (¾ inch) around the edges. Roll up, starting at the shorter edge, using the paper to help. Wrap in the paper, then in a sheet of foil. Twist the ends together tightly, leaving some space for the pudding to rise.

4. Transfer the pudding to the slow cooker pot and raise off the base slightly by standing it on 2 ramekin dishes. Pour boiling water into the pot to come a little up the sides of the pudding, being careful that the water cannot seep through any joins. Cover with the lid and cook on high for 4–5 hours or until the pudding is well risen.

5. Just before serving, melt the butter for the sauce in a pan. Stir in the flour, then gradually mix in the milk. Bring to the boil, stirring until smooth, and cook for 1–2 minutes. Stir in the parsley and season. Lift out the pudding, unwrap and cut into slices. Spoon over a little sauce.

Potato, Apple & Bacon Hotpot

———

SERVES 4 | PREPARATION TIME 20 minutes | COOKING TEMPERATURE low | COOKING TIME 9–10 hours

750 g (1½ lb) potatoes, thinly sliced
25 g (1 oz) butter
1 tablespoon sunflower oil
2 onions, roughly chopped
250 g (8 oz) smoked back bacon, diced
1 dessert apple, cored and sliced
2 tablespoons plain flour
450 ml (¾ pint) chicken stock (see page 7)
2 teaspoons English mustard
2 bay leaves
50 g (2 oz) Cheddar cheese, grated
salt and pepper

1. Preheat the slow cooker if necessary. Bring a large saucepan of water to the boil, add the potatoes and cook for 3 minutes, then drain.

2. Heat the butter and oil in a frying pan, add the onions and bacon and fry, stirring, for 5 minutes or until just beginning to turn golden. Stir in the apple and flour and season the mixture well.

3. Layer the potatoes and the onion mixture alternately in the slow cooker pot, ending with a layer of potatoes. Bring the stock and mustard to the boil in the frying pan, then pour into the slow cooker pot and add the bay leaves. Cover with the lid and cook on low for 9–10 hours.

4. Sprinkle the top of the potatoes with the cheese, lift the pot out of the housing using oven gloves and brown under the grill, if liked, then spoon into shallow bowls.

Cidered Pork with Sage Dumplings

SERVES 4 | PREPARATION TIME 25 minutes | COOKING TEMPERATURE low | COOKING TIME 9–11 hours

1 tablespoon sunflower oil

750 g (1½ lb) pork shoulder steaks, cubed and any fat discarded

1 leek, thinly sliced; the green and white parts kept separate

2 tablespoons plain flour

300 ml (½ pint) dry cider

300 ml (½ pint) chicken stock (see page 7)

200 g (7 oz) carrot, diced

1 dessert apple, cored and diced

2–3 stems of sage

salt and pepper

SAGE DUMPLINGS

150 g (5 oz) self-raising flour

75 g (3 oz) vegetable suet

1 tablespoon chopped sage

2 tablespoons chopped parsley

5–7 tablespoons water

1. Preheat the slow cooker if necessary. Heat the oil in a frying pan, add the pork a few pieces at a time until all the pieces are in the pan, then fry over a high heat until lightly browned. Lift out of pan with a slotted spoon and transfer to the slow cooker pot.

2. Add the white leek slices to the pan and fry for 2–3 minutes or until softened. Stir in the flour, then gradually mix in the cider and stock. Add the carrot, apple, sage and some salt and pepper. Bring to the boil, stirring. Pour the mixture into the slow cooker pot, cover with the lid and cook on low for 8–10 hours or until the pork is tender.

3. Make the dumplings. Put the flour, suet, herbs and a little salt and pepper into a bowl, mix together, then gradually stir in enough water to make a soft but not sticky dough. Cut into 12 pieces and roll into balls with floured hands. Stir the green leek slices into the pork casserole and arrange the dumplings on the top. Cover and cook, still on low, for 1 hour until they are well risen. Spoon into shallow bowls to serve.

Honey-glazed Gammon

SERVES 4 | PREPARATION TIME 20 minutes, plus soaking | COOKING TEMPERATURE high | COOKING TIME 5–7 hours

1 kg (2 lb) boneless smoked gammon joint, soaked overnight in cold water

1 onion, cut into wedges

300 g (10 oz) carrots, halved lengthways and cut into 2.5 cm (1 inch) chunks

500 g (1 lb) medium baking potatoes, scrubbed and quartered

2 bay leaves

6 cloves

½ teaspoon black peppercorns

900 ml (1½ pints) boiling water

GLAZE

2 tablespoons runny honey

2 teaspoons English mustard

1. Preheat the slow cooker if necessary. Put the gammon joint into the slow cooker pot. Tuck the vegetables around the sides, then add the bay leaves, cloves and peppercorns. Pour over the boiling water to just cover the gammon.

2. Cover with the lid and cook on high for 5–7 hours or until the gammon and vegetables are cooked through and tender. Lift the gammon out of the slow cooker pot and transfer to the base of a grill pan. Cut away the rind and discard.

3. Mix the honey and mustard together for the glaze, spoon over the top and sides of the joint, then add 3 ladlefuls of stock from the slow cooker pot to the base of the grill pan. Grill until the gammon is golden brown. Carve into slices and serve with the sauce from the grill pan and drained vegetables from the slow cooker pot. Accompany with steamed green beans, if liked.

Beef & Root Vegetable Hotpot

———

SERVES 4 | PREPARATION TIME 25 minutes | COOKING TEMPERATURE high | COOKING TIME 7–8 hours

1 tablespoon sunflower oil

750 g (1½ lb) braising beef, cubed

1 onion, chopped

2 tablespoons plain flour

600 ml (1 pint) beef stock (see page 7)

2 tablespoons Worcestershire sauce

1 tablespoon tomato purée

2 teaspoons English mustard

3 sprigs of rosemary

125 g (4 oz) carrots, diced

125 g (4 oz) swede, diced

125 g (4 oz) parsnip, diced

700 g (1 lb 6 oz) potatoes, thinly sliced

25 g (1 oz) butter

salt and pepper

1. Preheat the slow cooker if necessary. Heat the oil in a frying pan, add the beef a few pieces at a time until all the meat is in the pan, then fry over a high heat, stirring, until browned. Scoop the beef out of pan with a slotted spoon and transfer to the slow cooker pot.

2. Add the onion to the pan and fry, stirring, for 5 minutes or until softened and just beginning to turn golden. Stir in the flour, then gradually mix in the stock. Add the Worcestershire sauce, tomato purée, mustard and leaves from 2 sprigs of the rosemary. Season and bring to the boil, stirring.

3. Add the diced vegetables to the slow cooker pot. Pour the onions and sauce over them, then cover with the potato slices, arranging them so that they overlap and pressing them down into the stock. Sprinkle with the leaves torn from the remaining stem of rosemary and a little salt and pepper.

4. Cover and cook on high for 7–8 hours until the potatoes are tender. Lift the pot out of the housing using oven gloves, dot the potatoes with the butter and brown under a hot grill, if liked.

Beef & Guinness Puff Pies

———

SERVES 4–5 | PREPARATION TIME 40 minutes | COOKING TEMPERATURE low | COOKING TIME 8–10 hours

2 tablespoons sunflower oil, plus extra for greasing

750 g (1½ lb) lean stewing beef, cubed

1 onion, chopped

2 tablespoons plain flour, plus extra for dusting

300 ml (½ pint) Guinness

150 ml (¼ pint) beef stock (see page 7)

2 teaspoons hot horseradish sauce

1 tablespoon tomato purée

1 bay leaf

200 g (7 oz) cup mushrooms, sliced

salt and pepper

PASTRY

500 g (1 lb) ready-made puff pastry, thawed if frozen

beaten egg, to glaze

100 g (3½ oz) Stilton cheese (rind removed), crumbled

1. Preheat the slow cooker if necessary. Heat the oil in a large frying pan, add the meat a few pieces at a time until all the pieces are in the pan, then add the onion and fry over a medium heat, stirring, until the meat is evenly browned.

2. Stir in the flour, then gradually mix in the Guinness and the stock. Stir in the horseradish, tomato purée and a little salt and pepper, then add the bay leaf and bring to the boil. Transfer to the slow cooker pot and press the meat below the surface of the liquid. Cover with the lid and cook on low for 8–10 hours or until the meat is cooked through and very tender.

3. When almost ready to serve, preheat the oven to 200°C (400°F), Gas Mark 6. Discard the bay leaf and divide the beef mixture between 4 pie dishes, each about 450 ml (¾ pint). Mix in the mushrooms, then brush the top edge of the dishes with a little egg. Cut the pastry into 4 and roll each piece out on a floured surface until a little larger than the dishes, then press on to the dishes. Trim off the excess pastry and press your first and second fingers onto the pie edge, then make small cuts between them with a small knife to create a scalloped edge. Repeat all the way around each pie. Mark diagonal lines on top and brush with beaten egg. Put on a baking sheet and cook in the preheated oven for 30 minutes or until golden. Sprinkle with the Stilton and leave to melt for 1–2 minutes.

Sausages with Onion Gravy

———

SERVES 4 | PREPARATION TIME 15 minutes | COOKING TEMPERATURE low | COOKING TIME 6–8 hours

1 tablespoon sunflower oil

8 'gourmet' sausages, such as Sicilian or Toulouse

2 red onions, halved and thinly sliced

2 teaspoons light muscovado sugar

2 tablespoons plain flour

450 ml (¾ pint) beef stock (see page 7)

1 tablespoons sun-dried or ordinary tomato purée

1 bay leaf

salt and pepper

TO SERVE

large ready-made Yorkshire puddings

steamed carrots and broccoli

1. Preheat the slow cooker if necessary. Heat the oil in a frying pan, add the sausages and fry over a high heat for 5 minutes, turning until browned on all sides but not cooked through. Drain and transfer to the slow cooker pot.

2. Add the onions to the frying pan and fry over a medium heat for 5 minutes or until softened. Add the sugar and fry, stirring, for 5 more minutes or until the onion slices are caramelized around the edges.

3. Stir in the flour, then gradually mix in the stock. Add the tomato purée, the bay leaf and some salt and pepper and bring to the boil, still stirring. Pour over the sausages. Cover with the lid and cook on low for 6–8 hours or until the sausages are tender. Serve spooned into reheated ready-made large Yorkshire puddings accompanied with steamed carrots and broccoli.

Lamb Hotchpotch

———

SERVES 6 | PREPARATION TIME 20 minutes | COOKING TEMPERATURE low | COOKING TIME 8¼–10¼ hours

15 g (½ oz) butter
1 tablespoon sunflower oil
1 large onion, finely chopped
400 g (13 oz) lamb fillet, diced
175 g (6 oz) carrots, diced
175 g (6 oz) swede, diced
200 g (7 oz) potatoes, diced
1 leek, thinly sliced; keep white and green slices separate
50 g (2 oz) pearl barley
2–3 sprigs fresh rosemary
1.5 litres (2½ pints) lamb stock
salt and pepper

1. Preheat the slow cooker if necessary. Heat the butter and oil in a saucepan, add the onion and lamb and cook over a high heat until the lamb is browned and the onion is golden.

2. Stir in the carrots, swede, potatoes, white sliced leek, pearl barley and rosemary. Add the stock (or as much as you can get into the saucepan), season to taste and bring to the boil.

3. Transfer the mixture to the slow cooker pot (bring any remaining stock to the boil and add to the pot), cover and cook on low for 8–10 hours or until the pearl barley, vegetables and lamb are tender.

4. Add the sliced green leeks and cook on high for a further 15 minutes.

Slow-cooked Lamb Shanks

SERVES 4 | PREPARATION TIME 20 minutes | COOKING TEMPERATURE high | COOKING TIME 5–7 hours

2 tablespoons olive oil

4 lamb shanks, about 375 g (12 oz) each

625 g (1¼ lb) new potatoes, thickly sliced

2 onions, sliced

3–4 garlic cloves, finely chopped

300 ml (½ pint) white wine

150 ml (¼ pint) lamb stock

1 tablespoon runny honey

1 teaspoon dried oregano

75 g (3 oz) preserved lemons, cut into chunks

75 g (3 oz) green olives (optional)

salt and pepper

chopped parsley, to garnish

1. Preheat the slow cooker if necessary. Heat the oil in a large frying pan, add the lamb and fry, turning until browned on all sides. Arrange the potatoes in the base of the slow cooker pot, then put the lamb on top.

2. Add the onion to the pan and fry until softened, then mix in the garlic. Add the wine, stock, honey, oregano and a little salt and pepper and bring to the boil. Pour over the lamb, then add the lemons and olives, if using.

3. Cover with the lid and cook on high for 5–7 hours or until the potatoes are tender and the lamb is almost falling off the bone. Spoon into shallow bowls and sprinkle with parsley.

Mushroom & Chestnut Pudding

———

SERVES 4 | PREPARATION TIME 45 minutes | COOKING TEMPERATURE high | COOKING TIME 5–6 hours

SAUCE

15 g (½ oz) butter

1 tablespoon sunflower oil

1 onion, thinly sliced

1 tablespoon plain flour

300 ml (½ pint) vegetable
  stock (see page 7)

5 tablespoons ruby port

1 teaspoon Dijon mustard

1 teaspoon tomato purée

salt and pepper

PASTRY

300 g (10 oz) self-raising flour

½ teaspoon salt

150 g (5 oz) vegetable suet

2 tablespoons finely chopped
  rosemary leaves

about 200 ml (7 fl oz) water

FILLING

1 large flat mushroom, sliced

125 g (4 oz) chestnut cup
  mushrooms, sliced

200 g (7 oz) vacuum-packed
  prepared chestnuts

1. Preheat the slow cooker if necessary. Make the sauce. Heat the butter and oil in a large frying pan, add the onion and fry for 5 minutes. Stir in the flour, then mix in the stock, port, mustard and tomato purée. Season with salt and pepper, bring to the boil, stirring, then take off the heat.

2. Make the pastry. Mix together the flour, salt, suet and rosemary. Gradually add enough cold water to mix to a soft but not sticky dough. Knead lightly, then roll out on a floured surface to a circle 33 cm (13 inches) across. Cut a quarter segment from the circle of pastry and reserve.

3. Lift the remaining pastry into a greased 1.25 litre (2¼ pint) pudding basin and bring the cut edges together, overlapping them slightly so that the basin is completely lined with pastry, then press them together to seal. Layer the sauce, mushrooms and chestnuts into the basin, finishing with the sauce.

4. Pat the reserved pastry into a circle the same size as the top of the basin. Dampen the edges of the pastry in the basin with a little water and press the lid in place. Cover with oiled foil and dome the foil slightly. Tie in place with string, then put into the slow cooker pot. Pour boiling water into the slow cooker pot so that it comes halfway up the sides of the basin. Cover and cook on high for 5–6 hours.

186

179

181

182

Slow-baked Cakes & Puddings

———

Wicked Chocolate Pudding
Chocolate Spotted Dick
Pineapple Pudding
Steamed Pudding with Mango
Figgy Pudding
Christmas Pudding
Chocolate Sponge Pudding
Choc, Fruit & Nut Cake
Whisky Mac Cake
Easy Simnel Cake
Carrot & Banana Cake

Wicked Chocolate Pudding

———

SERVES 6 | PREPARATION TIME 20 minutes | COOKING TIME about 2 hours

75 g (3 oz) butter

150 g (5 oz) light muscovado
  sugar

finely grated rind of 1 orange

2 eggs

150 g (5 oz) self-raising flour

25 g (1 oz) cocoa powder

½ teaspoon bicarbonate of
  soda

100 g (3½ oz) milk chocolate,
  chopped

pouring cream or custard,
  to serve

SAUCE

125 g (4 oz) light muscovado
  sugar

75 g (3 oz) butter

4 tablespoons orange juice

50 g (2 oz) dates, stoned and
  chopped

1. Put the butter, sugar, orange rind and eggs in a large bowl, then sift in the flour, cocoa powder and bicarbonate of soda and beat well until creamy. Stir in the chocolate.

2. Grease the inside of a 1.2 litre (2 pint) pudding basin and line the base with nonstick baking paper. Turn the mixture into the basin and level the surface. Cover with a double thickness of nonstick baking paper and a sheet of foil, securing them under the rim of the basin with string.

3. Bring a 5 cm (2 inch) depth of water to the boil in a large pan. Lower in the pudding basin and cover the pan with a lid. Steam for 1¾ hours, topping up the water occasionally, if necessary.

4. Heat the sugar, butter and orange juice gently in a small pan until the sugar dissolves. Bring to the boil and boil for 1 minute. Stir in the dates and cook for 1 minute. To serve, invert the pudding on to a serving plate and pour the sauce over the top. Serve with pouring cream or custard.

Chocolate Spotted Dick

———

SERVES 6 | PREPARATION TIME 20 minutes | COOKING TIME 1¾–2 hours

75 g (3 oz) butter

75 g (3 oz) caster sugar

2 eggs, beaten

175 g (6 oz) plain dark chocolate drops

grated rind of 1 orange

1 tablespoon milk

1. In a large mixing bowl cream together the butter and sugar until light and fluffy. Beat in the eggs a little at a time, adding a teaspoon of the flour with each addition. Fold in the rest of the flour. Stir in the chocolate drops, orange rind and milk.

2. Spoon the mixture into a lightly greased 900 ml (1½ pint) pudding basin. Cover the pudding with a double thickness of greaseproof paper or foil. Make a pleat across the top to allow for rising and tie down securely with string.

3. Place the pudding basin in a saucepan of simmering water, ensuring that the water comes halfway up the sides of the basin. Cover with a tight-fitting lid and steam for 1¾–2 hours, topping up the water as necessary.

4. To turn the pudding out, remove the string and paper or foil. Loosen the upper edges of the pudding with a knife. Invert onto a warmed serving plate and serve warm with custard, cream or chocolate sauce (see page 180).

Pineapple Pudding

SERVES 4 | PREPARATION TIME 25 minutes | COOKING TIME 1½–2 hours

425 g (14 oz) can pineapple slices, drained	
15 g (½ oz) angelica	
125 g (4 oz) butter	
125 g (4 oz) caster sugar	
grated rind and juice of 1 lemon	
2 eggs	
150 g (5 oz) self-raising flour	

1. Lightly grease a 900 ml (1½ pint) pudding basin and arrange the pineapple slices around the base and sides. Place a piece of angelica in the centre of each slice of pineapple.

2. Put the butter, sugar and lemon rind in a mixing bowl and cream together until light and fluffy. Add the eggs, one at a time, adding a tablespoon of flour with the second egg. Beat thoroughly, then fold in the remaining flour with the lemon juice.

3. Carefully spoon the mixture into the pudding basin. Cover the pudding with a double thickness of greaseproof paper or foil. Make a pleat across the top to allow for rising and tie down securely with string.

4. Place the pudding basin in a saucepan of simmering water, ensuring that the water comes halfway up the sides of the basin. Cover with a tight-fitting lid and steam for 1½–2 hours, topping up the water as necessary. Turn into a warm serving dish and serve with custard.

Steamed Pudding with Mango

———

SERVES 6 | PREPARATION TIME 20 minutes, plus standing | COOKING TIME 1 hour 40 minutes

1 medium mango, cut into
  chunks

2 tablespoons vanilla syrup,
  plus extra for serving

125 g (4 oz) unsalted butter,
  softened

125 g (4 oz) caster sugar

1 teaspoon vanilla extract

2 eggs

175 g (6 oz) self-raising flour

4 tablespoons unsweetened
  dessicated coconut

1 tablespoon milk

1. Grease a 1.2 litre (2 pint) pudding basin and line the bottom with a circle of nonstick baking paper. Scatter the mango chunks in the prepared bowl and drizzle with the vanilla syrup.

2. Put the butter, sugar, vanilla, eggs and flour in a bowl and beat for 1–2 minutes until creamy. Stir in the coconut and milk, then spoon the mixture into the pudding basin. Level the surface.

3. Cover the bowl with a double thickness of pleated nonstick baking paper and secure under the rim with string. Cover with foil, tucking the edges firmly under the rim.

4. Put the bowl in a steamer or large pan. Half-fill the pan with boiling water and cover with a tight-fitting lid. Steam gently for 1 hour 40 minutes, topping up the water as necessary, then allow to stand for 10 minutes.

5. Invert the pudding on to a serving plate and drizzle with extra vanilla syrup.

Figgy Pudding

———

SERVES 6 | PREPARATION TIME 20 minutes, plus soaking | COOKING TIME 4 hours

250 g (8 oz) dried figs

250 g (8 oz) dates, pitted

125 g (4 oz) raisins

4 tablespoons brandy

250 g (8 oz) self-raising flour

175 g (6 oz) wholemeal
   breadcrumbs

175 g (6 oz) shredded suet

3 eggs, beaten

grated rind and juice of
   1 lemon

1. Chop the figs and dates and put them into a mixing bowl. Add the raisins and brandy. Stir well and leave to soak for at least an hour, but preferably overnight.

2. Add all the other ingredients to the fruit mixture and mix thoroughly. Grease a 1 litre (2 pint) pudding basin and put the fig mixture into this. Cover the pudding with a double thickness of greaseproof paper or foil. Make a pleat across the top to allow for rising and tie down securely with string.

3. Place the pudding basin in a saucepan of simmering water, ensuring that the water comes halfway up the sides of the basin. Cover with a tight-fitting lid and steam for 4 hours until firm, topping up the water as necessary.

4. Remove the paper or foil from the basin and invert the pudding onto a warm serving plate. Serve with cream or custard.

Christmas Pudding

SERVES 6–8 | PREPARATION TIME 20 minutes, plus soaking | COOKING TIME 8 hours

150 g (5 oz) shredded suet

2 tablespoons plain flour

200 g (7 oz) wholemeal breadcrumbs

200 g (7 oz) soft dark brown sugar

500 g (1 lb) mixed sultanas, raisins and currants

100 g (3½ oz) ready-to-eat dried apricots, chopped

2 teaspoons mixed spice

1 apple, grated

2 large eggs

4 tablespoons brandy

4 tablespoons apple juice

grated rind of 1 orange

1. Mix together all the ingredients in a large bowl, cover and leave to soak for 24 hours.

2. Spoon the mixture into a 1.2 litre (2 pint) pudding basin, cover with a piece of nonstick baking paper that has been folded with a pleat and secure with string, then cover with foil. Steam the pudding for about 6 hours, keeping the water topped up in the saucepan so that it does not dry out. When cooked, rewrap the pudding in nonstick baking paper and foil. Store in a cool place until Christmas time.

3. When ready to serve, steam the pudding for a further 2 hours as above. Serve hot with thick cream.

Chocolate Sponge Pudding

———

SERVES 4 | PREPARATION TIME 20 minutes | COOKING TIME 1½–2 hours

175 g (6 oz) self-raising flour

2 tablespoons cocoa powder

125 g (4 oz) butter

125 g (4 oz) caster sugar

2 large eggs

2 tablespoons milk

CHOCOLATE SAUCE

75 g (3 oz) plain dark
   chocolate

3 tablespoons golden syrup

2 tablespoons water

1. Sift the flour and cocoa together into a mixing bowl. Put the butter and sugar together in a separate bowl and cream together until light and fluffy. Beat in the eggs, one at a time, adding a tablespoon of the flour and cocoa mixture with the second egg. Fold in the remaining flour and cocoa and then mix in the milk.

2. Spoon the mixture into a lightly greased 1.2 litre (2 pint) pudding basin. Cover the pudding with a double thickness of greaseproof paper or foil. Make a pleat across the top to allow for rising and tie down securely with string.

3. Place the pudding basin in a saucepan of simmering water, ensuring that the water comes halfway up the sides of the basin. Cover with a tight-fitting lid and steam for 1½–2 hours, topping up the water as necessary.

4. To make the chocolate sauce, break the chocolate into pieces and place in a heatproof bowl set over a saucepan about one-third full of gently simmering water. Add the golden syrup and measurement water and melt, beating until smooth.

5. Turn the pudding out onto a warm serving plate and pour over the hot sauce. Serve immediately.

Choc, Fruit & Nut Cake

———

SERVES 12 | PREPARATION TIME 15 minutes, plus cooling | COOKING TIME about 2 hours

3 flaky chocolate bars,
chopped into 1.5 cm
(¾ inch) pieces

225 g (7½ oz) butter or
margarine

225 g (7½ oz) caster sugar

275 g (9 oz) self-raising flour

25 g (1 oz) cocoa powder

4 eggs

150 g (5 oz) hazelnuts, roughly
chopped

200 g (7 oz) plain dark
chocolate, chopped

225 g (7½ oz) raisins

cocoa powder or icing sugar,
for dusting

1. Cream together the butter or margarine and sugar. Add the flour, cocoa powder and eggs to the bowl and beat until smooth. Reserve half the pieces of flaky chocolate and 50 g (2 oz) each of the hazelnuts and plain dark chocolate. Fold the remainder into the cake mixture with the raisins.

2. Grease and line a 20 cm (8 inch) round or 18 cm (7 inch) square cake tin. Turn the mixture into the tin and scatter with the reserved chocolate and nuts. Bake in a preheated oven, 150°C (300°F), Gas Mark 2, for about 2 hours or until a skewer inserted into the centre comes out clean. Leave to cool in the tin. Serve lightly dusted with cocoa powder or icing sugar.

Whisky Mac Cake

———

SERVES 24 | PREPARATION TIME 40 minutes, plus soaking and cooling | COOKING TIME 3½–3¾ hours

1 kg (2 lb) luxury mixed dried fruit

4 tablespoons whisky

50 g (2 oz) ready-chopped glacé ginger

grated rind and juice of 1 lemon

300 g (10 oz) plain flour

2 teaspoons ground mixed spice

1 teaspoon ground cinnamon

250 g (8 oz) butter, at room temperature

250 g (8 oz) dark muscovado sugar

5 eggs, beaten

50 g (2 oz) pecan nuts, roughly chopped

TO DECORATE

11 glace cherry halves

11 pecan nuts

1. Put the dried fruit in a bowl with the whisky, glacé ginger, lemon rind and juice. Mix together, cover and leave to soak overnight.

2. Mix the flour with the spices. Beat the butter and sugar together in a mixing bowl until pale and creamy. Mix in alternate spoonfuls of beaten egg and flour until all has been added and the mixture is smooth. Gradually mix in the soaked fruit and chopped nuts until evenly combined.

3. Spoon the mixture into a 20 cm (8 inch) deep round cake tin, base and sides lined with nonstick baking paper, and spread the surface level. Arrange the cherry halves and pecans around the top edge. Bake in the centre of a preheated oven, 140°C (275°F), Gas Mark 1, for 3½–3¾ hours or until a skewer inserted into the centre comes out clean. Leave to cool in the tin for 30 minutes then loosen the edges, turn out on to a wire rack and peel off the lining paper. Leave to cool completely.

4. Decorate the cake with a strip of waxed paper tied round the cake with raffia, if liked. Store in an airtight tin for up to 2 weeks.

Easy Simnel Cake

SERVES 16 | PREPARATION TIME 25 minutes, plus cooling | COOKING TIME 2–2½ hours

175 g (6 oz) slightly salted butter, softened

175 g (6 oz) light muscovado sugar

2 teaspoons ground ginger

2 teaspoons ground mixed spice

3 eggs

225 g (7½ oz) plain flour

2 teaspoons vanilla extract

500 g (1 lb) luxury mixed dried fruit

500 g (1 lb) white or golden marzipan

1 egg white, lightly beaten, for brushing

yellow flowers, such as roses, or rose petals, to decorate

sifted icing sugar, for dusting

1. Beat together the butter, muscovado sugar, ginger, mixed spice, eggs, flour and vanilla in a bowl until smooth and creamy. Stir in the dried fruit until evenly combined. Spoon half the mixture into a greased and lined 18 cm (7 inch) round cake tin and level the surface.

2. Roll out half the marzipan on a surface lightly dusted with sifted icing sugar into a round the same size as the tin. Press into the tin and cover with the remaining mixture. Level the surface. Bake in a preheated oven, 150°C (300°F), Gas Mark 2, for 2–2½ hours or until a skewer inserted into the centre comes out clean. Leave to cool in the tin.

3. Transfer the cake to a baking sheet, peel off the lining paper and brush the top with the egg white. Roll out the remaining marzipan until slightly larger than the top of the cake. Lift over the cake and press down gently. Pinch the edges of the marzipan to decorate.

4. Brush with a little more egg white and cook under a preheated grill until lightly toasted, turning the cake if necessary to evenly colour. Leave to cool. Decorate with flowers or rose petals and dust with sifted icing sugar.

Carrot & Banana Cake

SERVES 14 | PREPARATION TIME 10 minutes, plus cooling | COOKING TIME 1 hour 40 minutes

175 g (6 oz) ready-to-eat dried apricots, roughly chopped

125 ml (4 fl oz) water

1 egg

2 tablespoons clear honey

100 g (3½ oz) walnuts, roughly chopped

500 g (1 lb) ripe bananas, mashed

1 large carrot, about 125 g (4 oz), grated

225 g (7½ oz) self-raising flour, sifted

TOPPING

150 g (5 oz) cream cheese

2 tablespoons lemon curd

1. Place the apricots in a small saucepan with the measurement water, bring to the boil and simmer for 10 minutes. Transfer to a liquidizer or food processor and blend to give a thick purée.

2. Put all the other cake ingredients in a large bowl and add the apricot purée. Mix well, then spoon into a greased and lined 1 kg (2 lb) loaf tin.

3. Bake in a preheated oven, 180°C (350°F), Gas Mark 4, for 1½ hours or until a skewer inserted in the middle comes out clean. Turn out on to a wire rack to cool.

4. Beat together the cream cheese and lemon curd and spread over the top of the loaf.

Index

———

Acknowledgements

——

Special photography © Octopus Publishing Group Limited/Stephen Conroy 2 (top right), 8 (bottom left), 22, 26, 28, 30 (top right, bottom right), 33, 34, 42, 45, 46 (top left, bottom left), 58, 64, 68, 78, 88, 95, 108 (top left, bottom right), 112, 126, 132 (top left, top right, bottom left, bottom right) 135, 137, 138, 141, 143, 144, 146, 148, 151, 153, 154, 157, 158, 160, 163, 164, 167, 168;/ Will Heap 30 (top left, bottom left), 37, 38, 41;/ David Munns 2 (bottom left), 54, 57, 75, 76, 116, 119, 122;/Lis Parsons 8 (top left), 12, 15, 49, 50, 53, 63, 70, 72 (bottom right), 83, 84, 87, 90, 93, 96,100, 105, 115, 124, 127, 128, 130, 187;/Craig Robertson 67;/Gareth Sambridge 170 (bottom left, bottom right) 173, 176, 181;/William Shaw 2 (top left, bottom right), 8 (top right, bottom right), 11, 16, 19, 21, 25, 27, 46 (bottom right), 60, 72 (bottom left), 79, 108 (top left), 111, 121,170 (top left, top right) 179, 183, 184;/Ian Wallace 46 (top right), 69, 72 (top left, top right), 80, 98, 108 (bottom right), 131.